Hipster
Business Models

Priceonomics

For information, please contact us:
info@priceonomics.com

ISBN-10: 0692340726
ISBN-13: 978-0692340721

Priceonomics Authors
Zachary Crockett
Rohin Dhar
Rosie Cima
Alex Mayyasi

Cover Design
Dan Abramson

CONTENTS

INTRODUCTION:
CONSIDER THE HIPSTER

Tight pants. Fake reading glasses. Beards. Irony. These are the requisite components of modern society's interpretation of the word *hipster*. Yet this was not always the case.

The word *hip* entered the American lexicon in 1902 as a term used to describe someone who was "aware" or "in the know" of new trends. Most etymologists believe the adjective derived from *hepicat*, a West African term meaning "one who has his eyes open."

After adopting its suffix (-stir) in the 1940s, a hipster came to be defined as a "character who [liked] hot jazz" or who frequented underground music venues. Soon, the term was used to identify the mainly white, upwardly-mobile youth who were "hip" to the African-American jazz scene.

Post-World War II, as a new literary scene emerged, hipsters were the young protagonists who explored America. "A generation of crazy, illuminated hipsters," wrote Jack Kerouac in 1957's *About the Beat Generation*, "is suddenly rising and roaming America, serious, bumming and hitchhiking everywhere, ragged, beatific, beautiful in an ugly graceful new way."

Today's hipsters are not thought of in such romantic terms. "In their modern incarnation," writes Christian Lorentzen of *Time Out New York*, hipsters are "essentially people who think of themselves as being cooler than America" – people who have "fetishized" old ideals. They are the butt of Internet jokes, the objects of ridicule, and the recipients of societal hatred.

This is all to say that the connotation of the word hipster is fluid – it has changed with the ebb and flow of various cultural movements. But the actual definition of the word has been unwavering: a hipster, according to Merriam-Webster Dictionary, is "a person who is unusually aware of and interested in new and unconventional patterns."

At its core, the word hipster has always referred to someone who embraces new ideas and tries to be different. One would think that this is a behavior we ought to celebrate, yet modern society chooses to load the word with negativity, and then use it as a slur against young people.

Perhaps it is time to reconsider the hipster.

The Hipster Business Model

If half of the hipster stereotype is a consumer who tries to show off how cool he is based on his tastes, the other half of the stereotype is The Maker – the person out hawking homemade cheese, sweaters for your beard, or steel-framed bicycles. In an effort to lampoon hipsters, most media accounts gloss over the sheer number of young people tinkering, creating, and finding novel ways to make a living. Instead, they prefer to discuss why hipsters don't listen to the band Coldplay, or to dissect their propensity to drink Pabst Blue Ribbon.

When author William Deresiewicz moved to Portland, Oregon, a place many consider the mothership of hipsterdom, he came face-to-face with hipster stereotypes. At every turn, he encountered young, tattooed, mustachioed adults. But Deresiewicz noted that the city's hipsters seemed different than prior generations of young people – and not just because of their fashion sense:

"Here's what I see around me, in the city and the culture: food carts, 20-somethings selling wallets made from recycled plastic bags, boutique pickle companies, techie start-ups, Kickstarter, urban-farming supply stores, and bottled water that wants to save the planet.

Today's ideal social form is not the commune or the movement or even the individual creator; it's the small business. Every artistic or moral aspiration — music, food, good works, what have you — is expressed in those terms."

What struck Deresiewicz most about living in Portland was that so-called "hipsters" wanted to create unique products, and also to sell them.

His observation is a trend we see playing out across America: young people are in Detroit fixing up real estate, in Burlington starting farms, and in San Francisco building tech companies. The "kids these days" aspire to be small business owners, startup founders, and makers. Just maybe, kids these days are alright.

Young people entering the workforce today have no expectation of long-term employment with a single company, a pension, or the government swooping in to provide economic salvation. Faced with the prospect of fierce competition with thousands of other applicants for jobs at large companies, many young people are instead opting to start their own businesses.

Luckily for them, there has never been a better time to a be a hipster businessman or businesswoman: the cost of starting a company and finding customers has plummeted in recent years. This book tells the stories of twenty-two entrepreneurs, some of whom you might call hipsters. These entrepreneurs are our main characters, but in every case, technology plays a supporting role.

Before the Internet, creating a business with national reach cost hundreds of millions of dollars and decades of work. At the dawn of the Internet, creating an online business cost tens of millions of dollars and took a few years. Now, it costs a few bucks a month and can be done in a couple of hours.

Those who are aware of these sinking startup costs can afford to quickly build businesses when an idea strikes. But there is a growing divide between the people who are armed with this knowledge and the people who assume starting a company is too expensive to be a realistic goal.

Some people think that there is only one way to start a business: protect an idea through a patent, get a loan to make a product, hire people who know how to make the product, get the product sold by retailers, spend money to advertise, and finally, find customers for said product.

And then there is the hipster business model: *Make a product you love so much that you'll make it yourself. See if anyone wants it. Try again.*

The entrepreneurs in this book *get started themselves* instead of waiting for people to help them. When they want to build apparel companies, they teach themselves how to sew. When they dream of producing toys, they learn how to use 3D printing software. When they don't know investors who will back their restaurant concepts, they open food trucks. All the while, they are guided by books, instructional videos, and intuition; only later do they move production to real factories, or hire lawyers.

The entrepreneurs in this book *sell*. They frequent public parks to see if anyone will buy their custom, typewritten stories. They use crowdfunding websites to raise money from customers before their products even exist. They post their ideas to massive web forums to gauge interest, or set up online shops the second they have a product to sell. Sales come first, not last.

Finally, the entrepreneurs in this book *try again.* In almost every instance, the first versions of their products don't work properly, or customers don't want them. Instead of giving up, they tinker – sometimes for years – until they get things right. They hit roadblocks and spend late nights anguishing over seemingly insurmountable obstacles, until one day, through sheer force of will, they make it. The ones who survive are the ones who don't quit.

It's Okay to Be Weird

Thirty-year-old Dan Abramson (left, in giraffe costume) explains to Bob how he raised over $100,000 on Kickstarter to create "little green army men doing yoga."

While technology has made it cheaper to build products and find customers, there is also a cultural trend at play: it is becoming more socially acceptable to pursue oddball ideas.

Today, food trucks are commended for their delicious food and nimble business models; a decade ago, we called them "roach coaches." Living in a van while operating a small business might now be seen as a "life-hack"; in the past, this lifestyle exemplified failure. A skilled person who makes fine leather wallets by hand is considered a craftsman; in prior eras, he could have likely been deemed a luddite.

New ideas usually look strange at first. Some of them mature into important institutions. Other ideas remain strange, and most just fade away. What is important is to cultivate a culture that celebrates new ideas in all their forms, especially new ideas about how to make a living; a culture where someone is encouraged, rather than criticized, for bringing his typewriter to the park to write stories, for making yoga action figures, or for sewing pockets on underwear.

The people and ideas in this book are all different. Some are young, some are old. Some are fashionable, others are not. Some have created serious businesses with hundreds of millions of dollars in revenue, while others are essentially performance artists who make very little money off their passion.

While each entrepreneur featured in this book embarked on his or her own unique quest, their stories share a common thread: like true hipsters, they were not afraid to try new things.

✦ ✦ ✦

THE MAN WHO GAVE
UNDERWEAR POCKETS

The idea struck on a hot Saturday morning in April.

Twenty-one year old Danieal Cormier woke up late in his apartment in New Brunswick, Canada, rose from bed and walked groggily to the kitchen to brew his coffee – all the while in his underwear ("Everyone does it," he tells us defensively). Then, as most weekend mornings go, he haphazardly began watching television, cleaning, and "just walking around from room to room."

While wandering, he'd hear his phone buzz and scramble to find it; every five minutes, he'd lose track of where it was. "Friends were texting me, I was doing e-mails, Facebook, and whatnot," Danieal recalls, "and I kept doing a hand motion to put the phone in my pocket – a pocket that wasn't there! Eventually, I realized, 'Okay, I need a freakin' pocket.'"

Danieal acquiesced and put on a pair of gym shorts with pockets, so he could carry his phone around the house. But after tasting the glorious freedom of walking around in his underwear, the now-clothed Canadian simply wasn't satisfied. "I said, 'Wait – I shouldn't have to put on a pair of shorts to have a pocket," he recalls. "That's just ridiculous."

"Then it hit me: underwear with pockets."

At the time, twenty-one year old Danieal Cormier was living a quiet existence. Every morning, he'd schlep to his 9-to-5 job as a sales and marketing assistant for a hotel chain. Every evening, he'd read, or watch television.

For years, he'd enviously watched his father, the owner and founder of a tile importing business, set his own schedule and make his own decisions. "I'd dream of starting my own business – of having my dad's autonomy," Danieal recalls. "I just had no idea what kind of business I'd start."

In the fervor of his new revelation, Danieal immediately went online to "buy a pair of underwear with pockets." Surely, he told himself, they must already exist. But the market for knickers with compartments wasn't stellar:

> *"There were only a few, and the selection sucked. One had these tiny little condom pockets. There was another, but the pockets were inside the underwear. So to access whatever was inside of it, you had to literally slip your hand into your crotch. That's not exactly what I wanted."*

"Right then and there, I just decided to make my own from scratch," he says.

There was one problem: Danieal had never sewn a stitch in his life or designed anything remotely resembling a product. But that didn't stop him. He got dressed, then went out and bought fabric and a sewing machine.

"Never use a sewing machine," he laughs. "That thing was impossible to figure out. It would jam all the time, the manual was like a dictionary. Just the simplest task of loading thread was incredibly difficult for a newbie." He started slow. Over several "agonizing" weeks, he taught himself how to sew a straight stitch line by utilizing YouTube, Wikipedia, and forums.

The first pair looked like hell.

"I still couldn't really hem properly," he says. "The outside looked passable, but the inside looked like...well, the quality just wasn't there, to put it nicely." At that point, it didn't much matter: his goal was just to make himself a pair or two. He was his only critic.

But as he continued to sew new pairs—each increasingly better than the last—he figured, "Why not sell them?"

***

Etsy, an online marketplace where artisans sell handmade goods, can be overwhelming. The site boasts 30 million users (both buyers and sellers) and some 7 million products. It's a vast sea of (mostly) awesome stuff made by (mostly) talented people. When Danieal joined, he felt like an aimless buoy.

"How could I make this semi-weird looking pair of underwear with pockets stand out? That was the question," he recalls. "I really figured I wouldn't make a single sale, or track any interest at all."

For the thrill of it, he posted his product, a red and white checkered pair with dual pockets. By enlisting his only marketing tool—a modest knowledge of SEO (or, how to optimize a site to garner traffic from search engines)—he generated somewhat favorable results for his shop in an Etsy search for "underwear with pockets."

When a week went by with no sales, Danieal began to question his new venture. Then, on day seven, a miracle: he sold his first pair of underwear—a lone red and white checkered set of boxers.

Over the next few months, "a dozen or so" more orders came in. "I was still working 9-to-5," Danieal reminds us, "so balancing work and underwear wasn't easy." It still took him nearly two hours to put together and sew a single pair—an enormous commitment for a $20 product. A few previous customers had also registered complaints about the underwear's stitching and sub-par comfort.

So Danieal, on a mission to deliver a high-quality product to his new customers, began to contemplate alternative methods of production. "I looked into sewing lessons so I could do it faster," he says. "I looked into Canadian seamstresses and factories—I really tried to find a local solution to do this in a cost effective way."

Eventually he decided that he'd have to take a different route to keep prices low: underwear with pockets was India-bound.

Finding a supplier overseas that met Danieal's criteria proved to be incredibly difficult.

Not only did he have "very high quality standards" for stitching and material, but he only wanted to produce an initial run of 100 pairs. "Most of them wanted to print 12,000 pairs," he says. "I was like, there's no way I'm making 12,000 pairs of pocketed underwear with like ten customers."

After searching through manufacturing websites for months, Danieal found a few people willing to produce smaller quantities. He narrowed the pool down to ten, then spent weeks calling them, getting samples, and asking "hundreds of questions."

"I wanted to see the quality, feel it, make sure it was what I wanted," he says. "Finally, I found the guy whose price was right, and who agreed to do 100 pairs."

Through this point, Danieal had done everything himself; he struggled with the idea of putting his "baby" in someone else's hands. But as he interacted with his contact in India, he accepted the prospect. "He was reliable and he was always there when I needed him," says Danieal. "I'm super lucky I found him."

The first 100 pairs came with a modest price tag of

$550. This was important because Danieal had elected to fund his underwear with pockets company out of pocket.

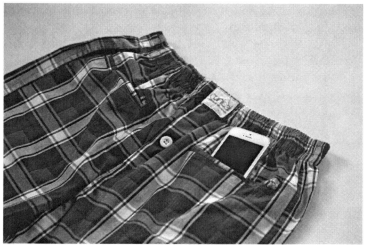

Danieal's final product, complete with iPhone pockets.

Fully stocked with 100 pairs by the end of March 2013, Danieal made another crucial business decision: he abandoned Etsy.

"When I saw the new undies, I decided that I wanted to be a brand—not just an independent artisan," he recalls. "I took everything off Etsy, and started to build my own website, my own company."

It was another intense process. Danieal, who had very minimal website building experience, programming knowledge, or design work under his belt, decided to do it without hired help. "Ever since I was a kid, I was on the computer fooling around," he says. "So instead of paying someone thousands of dollars to design a site, I just did it myself."

Behind the website's bells and whistles, Danieal also had a strategy: fake it 'til you make it. He presented his company, Danieal, as a large, established brand in the hopes of tricking people into believing it actually was one. "I set up the site to make it look like it was this official brand—and it turned into one because of that," he says.

In May 2014, with no customers, no followers, and no hype, Danieal went live.

Danieal quickly set out to tell the world about his pocketed underwear, starting with his home town. "I called a ton of shops and stores," he says. "And finally, the local hospital gift shop randomly agreed to carry the underwear."

It was an unlikely pairing, but with a bit of luck, it worked. One day in April, an executive producer at the CBC, Canada's biggest news outlet, spotted the underwear while leaving the hospital. The producer noticed it was made locally and contacted Danieal for a television and radio interview.

Then, says Danieal, "things took off like crazy." The company's name spread by word of mouth. A variety of other local shops offered to stock the underwear; soon, it was featured in a half-dozen stores all over Eastern Canada.

Danieal took advantage of the press and staged an "undie run" to benefit the hospital that had taken a chance on his product. More than 200 runners showed up—more than half of whom ran in Danieal underwear —with all proceeds going to charity.

***

From May to November of 2014, Danieal's company grew significantly. Today, his underwear is sold "coast to coast" in Canada and in a Mississippi "hipster clothing shop." He plans to expand further in the U.S.

In seven months, Danieal has sold roughly 2,500 pairs of underwear at $23 per pair, and he says online sales continue to rise each month. Since he does almost everything himself, his operating costs are incredibly low.

Danieal pays just $130 per year for website hosting and operation. It's his sole technology cost: Danieal built the site himself, designed his own logo, and does all the other design work. He does his own accounting, at an estimated expense of $8 per month, and though he outsources his packaging—a minimal cardboard wrapper—to another Canadian company, it only runs him about 45 cents per pair of underwear. He even learned to build his own store displays: two-by-four pieces of wood with "three underwear-filled baskets" hanging down. "I never built a birdhouse in my life," he says, "but I was somehow able to construct these giant things."

His biggest expense, running Facebook ads, pays for itself with sales. "We have great conversion rates," he claims, "and they've proven to be extremely effective."

As more people purchased Danieal's underwear, he began receiving feedback from the public that led him to reconsider the impact of his products.

"One customer emailed and said he likes my underwear because he can wear his insulin pump at night," says Danieal. "I never even considered it could have medical applications."

Another woman wrote to tell Danieal that her husband had just returned from a trip to Paris and had worn the underwear the entire time to avoid crafty European pickpockets. "Travel" is now included as one of the merits of the product on its webpage.

Due to high demand, Danieal also plans to release a line of boxer briefs in early 2015; to do so, he had to find another manufacturer who could work with the material. "It was almost like starting my company all over again," he says.

Looking back on his success so far, he's humbled.

"When I ordered those first 100 pairs of underwear, I thought I'd have them for the rest of my life," he laughs. "I never thought I would sell them—let alone this many pairs."

He's also become something of a local celebrity. "People will stop me in the mall sometimes and say, *'Hey are you the underwear guy? I'm a proud Danieal underwear wearer!'*" the inventor sheepishly admits.

"I guess we have a lot of enthusiastic wearers of underwear in Canada."

THE JELLYFISH ENTREPRENEUR

Alex Andon was elated when he received his first order to install a $25,000 jellyfish tank. He also had a problem: he didn't know much about jellyfish, and he didn't know how to make a jellyfish tank.

On a hunch that people would want to keep jellyfish as pets, Andon had created a test website and spent $100 on Google ads that targeted people who searched for the phrase "jellyfish tank." At the time, the only way to keep jellyfish at home was to pay a custom installer $10,000-$25,000. Lo' and behold, when Alex launched his business, his phone exploded with inquiries.

Four years later, Alex's company, Jellyfish Art, is the jellyfish pet market leader. In fact, it's pretty much the only company in the jellyfish pet market. Alex eventually ditched his custom installation business and developed a desktop jellyfish tank that brought the price of live jellyfish ownership down to $500.

Along the way, he launched one of the first popular Kickstarter campaigns, received funding from the Y Combinator startup incubator, and literally created a market out of nothing.

This is the story of Alex Andon and Jellyfish Art, the world's only jellyfish startup.

Who Wants a Pet Jellyfish?

In late 2007, Alex was two years out of college and itching to start a company – any kind of company at all. He lived with tech entrepreneurs in a house in San Francisco and worked as a lab technician at a struggling biotech firm.

As a marine biology major in college, Alex had noticed that jellyfish exhibits mesmerized aquarium visitors. "People seemed to have an obsessive infatuation with the jellies," he recalls. "Some people would sit in front of the tanks for hours staring at them." Since the jellyfish exhibits were so popular, he decided to explore whether there was a market for pet jellyfish.

Alex knew that jellyfish could survive in captivity and were fairly easy to catch in the wild. After briefly studying the design of jellyfish tanks at aquariums and conversing with breeders, he concluded that it was technically feasible to sell jellyfish to consumers.

While pet fish represent a roughly $2 billion a year market, the market for jellyfish is miniscule. One reason for this is that maintenance is tricky: if you put a jellyfish in an ordinary fish tank, it will instantly be sucked into the filter and die. In the 1960's, while attempting to safely house plankton, German oceanographer Wolfe Greve indirectly developed the key to housing jellyfish without killing them. Greve found that perfectly syncing a tank's water intake and outtake rate kept plankton (or jellyfish) from being liquified. He designed a tank with a perfectly balanced filtration system, and called it the "kriesel," which is German for "spinning top."

But according to Alex, no aquarium had a jellyfish exhibit until the 1990s. That's because they require a little stagecraft to be interesting. Most jellyfish look nondescript under normal light conditions. They're practically invisible until you shine LED lights on them or provide a background color, which is why all jellyfish tanks in aquariums involve some sort of lighting system. As Alex knew, and hoped more and more people would discover, if you create the right setting, jellyfish are stunning. When the Monterey Bay Aquarium took a chance and launched the first major jellyfish exhibit in the United States in 1992, it was a smash hit.

Alex knew jellyfish tanks were technically possible and potentially beautiful. But would people want them? To test demand, he created a basic website that advertised the services of his (at this point non-existent) custom jellyfish tank installation business called Jellyfish Art. Alex then started a Google Adwords advertising campaign that targeted search terms like "jellyfish tank" and "pet jellyfish."

Before he had spent $100 on Adwords, he made his first sale – a $25,000 custom jellyfish tank for a restaurant opening in Seattle.

The First Sale

Alex now faced the daunting challenge of delivering the tank to the restaurant. Based on research and talking to experts, Alex developed a general understanding of jellyfish tank construction. Daniel Pon, a home-aquarium-and-maintenance expert who now works at Jellyfish Art, remembers meeting Alex around this time:

> *"I had lunch with him and afterwards was like, 'This guy is in way over his head.' He doesn't know how basic things about a fish tank work and he's going to make a $25,000 jellyfish tank?"*

Alex describes the experience of installing his first jellyfish tank as "a complete disaster." Alex found a local aquarium builder to build the tank on his behalf, got a fishing permit and caught some jellyfish in a bay near San Francisco. He then had to get the tank and jellyfish up to Seattle for installation while the restaurant was under construction:

> *"A little before Christmas, a friend and I drove the tank up to Seattle. It was bad. It was filled with water and jellyfish so the truck weight was three times its legal payload."*

> *"It started snowing really hard on the way up. We had to put chains on our tires. I'd never done that before. We went through three sets of chains."*

In hindsight, it would have been easier to ship an empty tank: the jellyfish died during the drive, and Alex later had to replace them. The main issue, however, was setting up the jellyfish tank in the restaurant: to properly do so, Alex worked for five days straight with a construction company and slept on-site every night.

Alex got the tank installed in time for the restaurant's opening, but it had a few hiccups. One day a pipe broke and dumped 100 gallons of water into the restaurant. The annoyed restaurant owners were surprisingly understanding: they still use the tank today, though it now houses regular fish.

The Desktop Jellyfish Tank

With one customer under his belt, Alex decided to go into the jellyfish business. His website and advertising campaign kept getting him customers who wanted custom jellyfish tanks installed. At the same time, the biotech company Alex worked for, which had been hit hard by the recession, asked for volunteers to leave the company in exchange for severance. Alex left the company and committed to his jellyfish business.

The custom jellyfish tank installation business was

brutally difficult, but Alex quickly earned an under-standing of tank design and the aquarium and pet supply industry. He soon realized that, in order to grow, he needed to build an affordable jellyfish tank. Over the course of a year, Alex had finished only three custom installations. The market for $25,000 tanks was too small and too labor-intensive to scale. Instead of selling installation services, Alex needed to sell a product.

In February of 2009, Alex put up another page on his website offering a desktop jellyfish tank for around $500. It included a photoshopped image of a tank that didn't quite exist yet. He also got his big break: *The New York Times* profiled him in an article about people starting businesses after losing their jobs during the recession. The article put Alex on the map as "the jellyfish entrepreneur."

A few months later, the first version of Alex's desk-top jellyfish product was ready. It was a bit of a Franken-aquarium, hacked together from various off-the-shelf aquarium parts. But it worked. It kept the jel-lyfish alive, made them look pretty, and cost around $500.

Sales of the desktop jellyfish tank took off. The *New York Times* article ushered in a wave of articles by other publications about Jellyfish Art. And visitors drawn to the site by the press could now actually buy the tank. Jellyfish Art began to look like a real business with a scalable product.

The increase in sales, however, exposed a critical problem that Jellyfish Art struggles with to this day. Alex had succeeded in making an affordable jellyfish tank that people wanted, but he still needed a reliable supply of jellyfish.

***

The Jellyfish Supply Chain

When Alex started Jellyfish Art, he caught the creatures himself. After being rewarded with multiple stings and infrequent catches, Alex began his search for a jellyfish supplier:

> *"Basically, I just asked everyone. One local aquarium gave me a list of a few people who might be able to help. One of them worked out."*

For one year, the supplier, who lived on a tropical island, would put 500-1000 jellyfish in styrofoam coolers and ship them via commercial carrier to San Francisco. This meant they flew in the cargo section of regular passenger planes. Alex monitored the flight online and picked up the jellyfish at San Francisco Airport like you might pick up your in-laws.

Alex kept the jellyfish stock at the company's warehouse and office in the Potrero Hill neighborhood of San Francisco.

When Jellyfish Art receives an order, it ships jellyfish to the customer by FedEx overnight. Jellyfish Art guarantees that they arrive alive. Jellyfish can survive 48-72 hours in transit, so they usually survive even if there is a delay.

The supply chain worked this way for a year. One day, however, the tropical supplier went to his fishing spot and couldn't catch a single jellyfish. All of them were gone. Every week, he checked out the same spot. And every week, he went home empty-handed.

But Jellyfish Art survived. Thanks to the company's increased market exposure, Alex found a new supplier in Europe who provided just enough jellyfish. If you breed jellyfish to sell, Jellyfish Art is the only game in town.

First Jellyfish, Then the World

After a year of selling another company's fish tank retrofitted with his own filtration system, Alex decided Jellyfish Art should develop its own tanks. Armed with the knowledge to do this himself, Alex designed Jellyfish Art's signature product, the desktop jellyfish tank, on a dinner napkin:

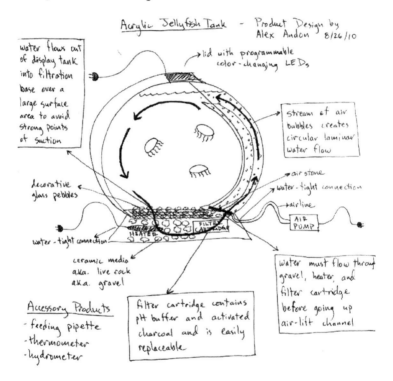

It took a year to go from sketch to production. In March of 2011, Andon unveiled his barely-functioning prototype at the Global Pet Expo, the largest trade show in the pet industry. Companies with huge market-ing budgets typically dominate the expo. Alex and his team had the smallest booth, but they won Best New

Product of the year in the aquarium category.

After winning at the Expo, Jellyfish Art started moving quickly. Alex found a Chinese manufacturer for the tanks and secured a small business loan to fund initial production. Alex also heard about Kickstarter, a website where potential customers could fund projects and inventions they wanted to see created. He figured it could be a good way to get orders and fund manufacturing.

In August of 2011, his company launched a Kickstarter campaign, with the aim of raising $3,000 in pre-orders. For the first few days of the campaign, sales trickled in. Then, when rap artist Jermaine Dupri tweeted about Alex's project, activity spiked and the campaign took off. Blog coverage soon segued into television and radio interviews: by month's end, Jellyfish Art had raised $162,917.

After "blowing up on Kickstarter," Alex decided to apply to Y Combinator, the technology startup incubator and investment firm. His application proposed using jellyfish as a beachhead to become the "Amazon.com for pets." Y Combinator accepted Jellyfish Art into the Y Combinator Winter 2012 batch.

Growing Pains

After a meteoric rise in the fall of 2011, gravity set in during the winter of 2012. As Alex started the Y Combinator program, he realized that the "Amazon.com for pets" idea wasn't a very good one. Shipping around live animals in boxes is a niche industry with low margins. The big money is in dogs and cats, and they aren't exactly portable or bought in bulk.

After considering creating a database of dog breeders, Alex decided against the idea. His existing jellyfish business offered no advantages for starting a breeder-matching service. Given the decision between starting from scratch in a new field or sticking with jellyfish, he chose jellyfish.

During Y Combinator, Alex felt pressure to show strong revenue growth on his sales chart. After he shipped the jellyfish tanks to his Kickstarter backers, he launched a sale on Fab.com, a then-popular flash sale site. The sale on Fab.com was the company's largest ever source of sales, but it came at a cost. Jellyfish Art offered the same discount on Fab as it offered its Kickstarter backers, who were livid that they received the same treatment after funding the business and putting up with a six month wait. Overnight, Jellyfish Art annoyed some of its biggest supporters.

In the wake of massive sales growth from Kickstarter and Fab, Alex started hiring staff and investing in systems needed to grow quickly. Sales kept increasing and it was unclear just how massive the business could become. Alex explains:

> *"As fast as money was coming in the door, it was flying out. We also had no idea how high the sales would go, whether we should be bracing for more growth or planning for stability. It turned out our product was too expensive for many of the large retail chains that originally showed interest, so sales eventually leveled out."*

As time went on, it became clear that sales wouldn't continue to rise as quickly as they had in the past few months. What was previously a profitable business was now operating at much thinner margins – a result of spending money like a high-growth startup. As sales started to flatten out, Alex let half of his staff go.

***

Living in San Francisco with tech entrepreneurs heavily influenced Alex. He tried to turn Jellyfish Art into a technology business, and he still aspires to create a massive, fast-growing technology startup some day.

Over the last year, however, sales at Jellyfish Art have been strong but flat. Anyone in the world willing to pay $500 for jellyfish buys the product from Jellyfish Art. The company dominates the market – no competitors have emerged, and jellyfish-related Google searches inevitably turn up the Jellyfish Art website or articles about the company. But with almost 100% market share, it's hard to increase sales.

In order to grow, Jellyfish Art needs to find a bigger market. According to Alex, the company needs to roll out a $100 tank, opening up a much larger market and getting shelf space in large retailers. Jellyfish Art has already built a low-cost jellyfish tank, but the company can't release it until it finds a way to source enough jellyfish. Jellyfish Art currently sells every jellyfish it can find.

The whole fate of the business hangs on whether the company can breed jellyfish in-house. Jellyfish Art is getting better at it, but right now the company breeds only 10% of its supply and buys the other 90%. When the company nails the process, it can lower prices and grow again.

Although Jellyfish Art does not resemble a technology startup, Alex Andon followed an entrepreneurial playbook that even Steve Jobs would've appreciated. At every stage in Jellyfish Art's evolution, Alex has sold well ahead of his capabilities. He sold a $25,000 tank he didn't know how to build. He sold a jerry-rigged version of another company's product before he could build his own desktop tank. He entered a barely-functioning prototype of his tank in a trade show and won first prize. Alex was a "fake it till you make it" entrepreneur par excellence.

The home jellyfish market is small, but Jellyfish Art both created it and dominated it. Alex thought he could turn Jellyfish Art into a tech business, but he couldn't. At the end of the day, it remains a jellyfish business. But that's still pretty awesome.

THE VAN WITH NO PLAN

In the crisp November dawn, brothers Josh and Matt Monthei loaded the last of their gear into the back of a white Ford Econoline van, gave each other a final nod of approval, and hit the road.

The brothers had enough gas to get them somewhere – anywhere. They'd neatly packed their few possessions beneath the van's pull-out bed: skateboards, t-shirts, a couple pairs of scuffed shoes. A windshield repair kit – their business and livelihood – lay tucked inside the overhead storage bin.

They had no idea where they were going, and it didn't matter.

They were in a van, with no plan.

Rough Roots

Josh and Matt Monthei led a mobile childhood. The brothers' mother, who raised the boys as a single parent, sometimes struggled to find work. When she found it, it often required loading up the family car and moving to a new place.

The family bounced around a slew of states – Texas, California, Colorado, and Nevada – before settling in Butte, Montana. When Josh graduated from high school, he packed his bags and moved to California to work in the Department of Labor's Job Corps, a free program for low-income teenagers looking to accrue vocational skills. Three years later, Matt dropped out of boot camp for the Montana National Guard and joined his brother in California.

In Sacramento, the brothers came across a man who lived in a mall parking lot and made a modest living repairing windshield cracks. When the brothers inquired about work, the man offered them jobs. The labor was tedious. It involved long days spent mulling around gas stations and parking lots under a hot sun, which usually proved unfruitful. Using a tiny plunger, they'd inject tiny cracks with UV-cured resin – a repair that takes about 10 minutes.

Their first boss also proved to be incredibly "shady." "The guy was really, really suspicious," Matt tells us. "Small windshield repairs are covered under most car insurance plans, so he was running this complete scam where he'd trick people into paying extra."

The brothers left to work for another windshield repair company, but this venture, operated by "a just plain crazy dude," was equally mismanaged. Again, the brothers left – this time to pursue an opportunity their close friend had come across in nearby Davis, California. As Matt recalls:

> *"This schoolteacher was looking for an investment. So, we told him about our plan – to start our own windshield repair business – and he actually put up $50,000 for us to do that."*

The collaboration proved fruitful. After a year and a half of hard work, the business had generated $150,000 in profit, almost entirely from the hard work of the two brothers, who each saw a small chunk of the money. But, like their previous work in windshield repair, this too fell through. Their success inspired a lot of local competition that hurt business. "By that time, everyone was doing windshield repairs," says Josh.

"The business was really crowded, and we weren't doing as well."

The investor shut down the business while it was ahead, and left the brothers without work. "The investor felt he'd made his money, and was done," says Josh. Worse, just two weeks earlier, when they felt securely employed, the brothers had purchased a work van, a white 1992 Ford Econoline E-250, for $600 from a family friend. "We kind of just asked ourselves, 'Well, what the hell do we do with this monstrosity now?'" Matt recalls.

Then one night, over a beer, the brothers reasoned: If we can walk into a parking lot and make enough money to cover rent, why can't we do the same while living on the road and paying for gas?

With no specific plan and $400 in their pockets, Matt, Josh, and their little dog Molly hit the road.

On the Road

The van had "come together perfectly" for the brothers. "The guy who'd had it before us used it for bass fishing trips," says Matt, "so it was already converted." With hardwood flooring, carpets, built-in storage, and a futon that folded into a bed, they didn't have to modify the van at all to start living in it.

They drove down the coast, first stopping in San Francisco, and then moving on to Los Angeles, where they set up their first windshield repair stand in a parking lot. Their business model, which remains the same today, was simple: Give out "free" windshield repairs, and let the customer pay what he or she thinks is fair for the service.

"We just went out and did these repairs not expecting to make a whole lot," says Matt. "It really varied a ton at first." Most people paid the brothers $15 to $20, some gave "a couple quarters," and one time, someone gave them a $100 bill.

The brothers cut eastward across the deserts of Nevada, Arizona, and New Mexico, setting up shop in each town they passed through. They had minimal expenses: the van got surprisingly good gas mileage on the highway, and its interior served as a mobile motel room each night. The brothers describe themselves as "stealth parkers"; by parking inconspicuously on public streets, they never had to pay for parking. Food was by far their biggest expense.

"We eat a lot," jokes Matt. "That's no surprise to anyone who knows us."

Even so, they spent an average of only $100 per week on groceries – an amount amply covered by their windshield-repair profits – by purchasing cheap items like rice, oats, and lentils in bulk.

Josh and Matt Monthei enjoying a remote stretch of land

According to Matt, their work was not appreciated in a few locations:

> *"Texas literally had a cop set up in every Walmart or big store's parking lot. As we were going around doing repairs, they thought we were breaking into cars. We got pulled over and had our van extensively searched, and they kicked us out."*

"I shit you not," he laughs, "we left Texas so fast!"

But most everywhere else, the siblings' kindheartedness and tenacity paid off. "Matt and I are openminded – we're not shy one bit," declares Josh. "We'll talk to anyone, and on the road, we build connections really fast." As they snaked their way through Louisiana, Arkansas, and Mississippi, this often led to additional odd jobs.

"We'd find a local, and say, 'We just got into town with no money and no plans – do you know of any work?'" says Josh. "They'd show us love, and hook us up with opportunities." The brothers gratefully cleaned bathrooms, worked in bagel shops, and performed hard labor. The jobs allowed them to continue their mobile lifestyle and supplemented their windshield repair business on slow days.

It also allowed them to pursue volunteer work, which eventually became a staple of their itinerary. The first opportunity arose in Memphis, Tennessee, says Matt:

> *"We were looking on Craigslist for work, and saw that a church needed help being rebuilt. It was just this group of people trying to self-fund the construction – and we dig it when someone has a passion to do something and they self-fund it. We*

*stayed there all day, tore out walls, and
helped clean up."*

The brothers pulled into New York just a few
months after Hurricane Sandy, and they continued
their volunteer work on Staten Island. With a small
team of social workers, they spent a week in hazmat
suits removing mold from flooded homes. "It was a
wasteland," says Josh. "Boats and trees were everywhere, houses were in total disrepair, the streets were
caked in grime. But it was totally rewarding."

In North Carolina, the brothers went on a charity
torrent, raising money to buy Christmas presents for a
family in need, planting vegetables at Goodwill's
charity farm, and working at an animal shelter. "[The
Monthei brothers] have been instrumental," Teresa
Nichols, of Safe Haven Shelter for Cats told a local
paper in Raleigh. "They have cleaned, they have moved,
they have packed food, and they have made an impact
on us and our volunteers." In exchange for their hard
work, the brothers received enough food to feed their
"road dog," Molly, for the rest of the year.

Through their volunteer work, Josh and Matt made
connections that led to paid-work. A friend from the cat
shelter hooked them up with a stone and tile company,
where they worked for a month and made "really great
money." In Florida, a charity event led to an employment opportunity at Universal Studios. "I worked at the
Captain America diner," Matt says, with a chuckle, "and
Josh worked at Circus McGurkis."

Even when the duo made good money, they worked
every day. "We like to keep ourselves busy," says Matt.
"And besides, we're horrible with money; as we got it,
there were always a million things we decided we
needed for the van."

When Things Go Wrong

Running a business on the road isn't all rainbows. As Matt explains, you're highly dependant on your vehicle, and if something happens to it, it can eat deep into your finances.

In New York, just four hours before the ball dropped on New Year's Eve, the brothers' van broke down in the middle of Union Square in Manhattan. As hordes of eager spectators rushed to the city center, the brothers sweat bullets.

"I kid you not – it was just hours before the ball dropped," says Matt. "By some stroke of luck, we called a mechanic on Craigslist who was just a few blocks away. He pretty much saved our asses."

After tinkering beneath the van for a few minutes "banging on shit," the mechanic emerged and told them their fuel pump was out. He hacked together a temporary solution, and the brothers made it to New Jersey before the van broke down again in a gas station parking lot. It remained there for two weeks while the brothers repaired enough windshields to afford the $480 repair. Optimism, says Matt, is the key to survival on the road. That, and a mobile business to pay for unexpected mishaps.

> *"Everything happens for a reason," Matt says. "And with some means of making money, the worst situations become the best – it's just another opportunity to meet people and do something nice."*

But some setbacks had no silver lining. In North Carolina, just after wrapping up an evening of volunteer work at the animal shelter, the brothers invited a new "friend" into their van. Minutes into their conversation, the police rolled up and searched the man's car, which was parked behind the van. When he saw his car being searched, the man conspicuously bolted. The cops eventually left, and the brothers drove off, only to make a terrifying discovery 100 miles down the road

"We found two guns stashed in the van loaded with magazine clips," recalls Matt. "First dumpster we saw, we got rid of them, and haven't really talked about it since."

Life in a Bus

After nine months on the road covering 40,000 miles and 32 states, Josh and Matt returned to Portland, Oregon, for their little brother's birthday on August 9. "It's the only day of the year we'd never miss," says Josh.

The brothers' durable van had sustained some serious wear and tear. On a whim, they searched Craigslist for a replacement vehicle, and they discovered an ad for a junk sale that included "a bunch of large vehicles." They contacted the seller, who lived way out in the boonies, and he invited them over to check out his selection.

"The guy was a total hoarder," says Matt. "The property was just packed with all kinds of stuff – RVs, boats, trailers – all in horrible shape."

And then they saw it, partially hidden behind a tall pile of junk: a 26-foot long 1993 Ford Econoline bus. The brothers fell in love and offered the man a trade: their van for his ratty, old bus. The hoarder claimed that the van was worth $1,500 and the bus $4,500, but after some contemplation, he told Josh and Matt that they could work 250 hours on his property to make up the difference.

For five weeks, the brothers cleared junk, repaired roofs, and moved heavy machinery – all the while fixing up the damaged bus and getting it road-ready:

*"It was in horrible condition. We literally
stripped it out completely. Then, we took a
pile of scrap wood he had on his property
and repurposed it into L-shaped bunk
beds, a little table, and a couch that folded
into a bed."*

The brothers used the skills they had accrued
working odd jobs on the road. What little they didn't
know, they learned through YouTube videos and tutorials. By the time they left the man's property, their new
bus had flooring, carpeting, a heater, storage units, and
mattresses installed.

"It's like we saved that bus's life," says Matt. "It was
sitting on his property rotting away. Even our mom
said, 'Don't buy that piece of crap.' But we did, and by
the time we were finished, it had a second life on the
road with us."

The Monthei brothers' bus on the road

With their new vehicle, the brothers took off on the second leg of their journey: a tour up and down the West coast. In Seattle, in a coup of bartering, they earned a trip on a yacht.

"We were determined to go on a boat, because we'd never been on one before, so we called over 30 companies offering to work in exchange for one ride. Finally, this one captain agreed, on one [condition]: we had to wax his yacht.

After waxing his yacht on Monday, he agreed to take us out on Friday. In the days between, we went around the piers asking if people needed their boats waxed. We let them pick their own prices and never got paid under $300 per boat. So by week's end, we'd made $1,500 and got to go for a cruise in a sweet yacht!"

In Hollister, California, during a Fourth of July rally, the duo managed to make $1,600 in one weekend by serving as the festival manager's "right-hand men." Using skills they'd learned doing volunteer work, they ran the stalls, supplied the beer gardens, managed a large event staff, and set up performance stages.

They would need the money later on. In the following five months, the bus broke down three times, and it proved difficult to find mechanics willing to work on the behemoth for cheap.

"Our air compressor broke, and if that breaks in a bus, you have no suspension. The whole thing slams to the ground," says Josh. "For two months, we went to a gas station every morning and manually aired up the thing to keep it running."

At times like these, the brothers questioned their loyalty to their fickle travel partner. "We loved and hated that bus so much at the same time," laughs Matt. Eventually the bus gave out. By August of 2014, when they once again returned for their little brother's birthday, the bus was in terrible shape.

Once again, they made a trade:

> *"We were thinking about spending all this money fixing it, but we showed it to couple who were interested in it first and they loved it. They had a Mercedes Sprinter van and made a straight trade – even though the Sprinter was worth $16,000 and our bus was only worth $9,000."*

At 23 miles per gallon, the brothers' new Sprinter was better suited to the road than the old 14 MPG bus. But unlike their first van, it had to be modified. "It was previously used as a dog-grooming van," laughs Matt. "When we got it, there was a 300-pound dog bathtub in it that we had to take out. That wasn't fun." They worked at a glass studio for a few weeks in exchange for lumber, which they used to build overhead storage and install hardwood floors.

Today, they remain on the road, and their third vehicle is going strong.

The 'No Plan' Philosophy

Occasionally, people who don't approve of Josh and Matt's lifestyle will say, "Ew, you guys live in a van," but it doesn't bother the duo. On the road, they find solace reveling in the cracks of life most people don't see.

Though they travel without a plan, the brothers don't consider themselves aimless roamers. They're mobile businessmen – hustlers with big ambitions and big hearts.

"Following the 'no plan' plan brightens you up," Matt tells us over the phone, while preparing chili in a parking lot somewhere in Washington. "When you have no plan, you have no expectations – and when you have no expectations, everything that happens to you is unexpectedly wonderful

THE ROVING TYPIST

In the summer of 2012, CD Hermelin packed his bags and moved to New York City to enter a master's program.

CD needed to work while he earned his degree, so every day, he sent out his resume to restaurants, offices, real estate companies and anywhere else that would employ him while he went to school at night. After sending dozens of resumes without results, CD started to feel down. He was also running out of money.

To make ends meet, CD fell back on what he did best: he wrote stories. One afternoon, he took his typewriter into New York's public parks and armed himself with a small sign that read, "One-of-a-kind, Unique Stories While You Wait. Sliding Scale – Donate What You Can!" Improbably enough, people started lining up to pay CD money for his stories. Life was good. CD was writing, delighting people with his custom stories, and making a decent amount of money as the "Roving Typist."

One day, a bypasser snapped a photo of CD and posted it on the Internet, which changed everything. The picture captured CD sitting on a park bench using a typewriter, but it cropped out the sign that indicated he was doing this as a business. Instead, he looked like someone who sat outside using a typewriter, presumably for the sake of looking contrarian.

The collective intelligence of the Internet knew

exactly how to characterize CD: he was a "stupid hipster" who used his typewriter to be "ironic" or to "get attention." As Internet commenters rushed to judge CD solely based on this picture, the truth was lost: CD was just trying to make a living in the city.

The Birth of the Roving Typist

Before living in New York, CD lived in San Francisco. While out in the city's Mission District, he saw a street typewriting performer offering to write custom poems for a donation. Instantly, CD knew he wanted to do this too. He approached the street poet and asked permission to replicate what he was doing. "Go for it," the poet responded, "but pick a different neighborhood."

A week later, CD picked up a working typewriter at a garage sale and headed to Union Square, a busy tourist and shopping destination in the center of San Francisco. With great anticipation, he sat next to his sign and offered to type stories for people in exchange for donations.

It did not go well. A nearby cellist screamed at CD for intruding his space; a light drizzle wet his typewriter and paper. Worst of all, in CD's words, the stories he wrote, "just weren't very good." Discouraged, CD shelved his idea as a "failed experiment."

While CD's attempt at street-typing didn't work, he threw himself into other writing adventures. With his roommate Max, he launched a website called A Story and a Picture. Max, who had an interest in photography and web development, would take an interesting picture and then CD would write a one-thousand-word fictional story to accompany it. Through this site, CD wrote about 75 stories.

Around this time, CD maintained an online journal and timed each day how fast he could write. After a four years of practice, he could write a 1,000-word story (roughly four pages in a Word document) in a mere nine minutes.

Moving to New York

In 2012, as CD struggled to find a "real job" in New York, he reconsidered his experiment in street-typing. By this point, he was pretty decent at writing stories on demand. So, e figured, "Why not dust off the old type-writer and give it another shot?"

His first attempt in New York did not go much better than his try in San Francisco. After four hours in New York's Union Square park, CD made just $12. His round-trip subway fare was $8, so after eating a $2 slice of pizza, he came home with only $2 in his pocket.

While it wasn't lucrative, the experience was more enjoyable than his attempt in San Francisco. He'd grown quite good at writing on-demand thanks to his years of practice, and people seemed delighted to read his stories. Ultimately though, Union Square proved too crowded with other street performers. CD didn't stand out enough to make money.

So CD went on a tour of New York City parks, trying to find somewhere he could generate a decent income. He found he was especially popular at parks with lots of children who wanted stories about Pokemon and Dragon Ball Z, but these customers didn't have much money. It was on a quiet bench in one of the city's newest parks – the High Line – where CD finally found success.

Opened to the public just the year before, the High Line was a park built on an abandoned, 1.45 mile elevated railroad platform. Because it was new and a unique urban experience, the High Line was a major attraction for tourists and local New Yorkers alike. Moreover, the park is essentially one long, straight line. So any visitor walking the length of the park would have to walk past CD.

CD took a seat on a park bench, trying to take up as little space as a possible. Park rangers sometimes turned away unauthorized street performers, and he didn't want to draw their attention. He also made sure to space himself far away from other performers. Then, once again, he put out his sign offering to type stories for donations.

This time, he made money!

In his first High Line test, he made $80 in just four hours – vastly preferable to the "almost nothing" he'd made elsewhere. Moreover, he actually enjoyed it. Even after finding a "regular job" at a real estate office, CD returned to the High Line twice a week. On average, he made $120 over what was typically a very intense four-hour stretch of story telling. Sometimes he'd strike out and only make a few bucks; other times, he made over $200. As recalled by CD, it worked out to be a pretty good job:

> *"On the High Line with my typewriter, all the joy of creating narrative was infused with a performer's high—people held their one-page flash fictions and read them and laughed and repeated lines and translated [them] into their own languages, right in front of me. Perhaps other writers would have their nerves wracked by instant feedback on rough drafts, but all I could do was smile."*

CD was writing, making money, and figuring out how to get by in New York City. Then, as quickly as he'd carved out his niche, he became the most hated hipster in America.

Look at This Fucking Hipster

It started harmlessly enough, when someone snapped a picture of CD sitting on a park bench typing a story for several young women. The individual then added a caption to the photo, "Spotted on the High Line," and posted it to Reddit, a vast online forum that has a way of making things spread.

There was one problem. CD's sign was entirely cropped out of the picture. So, too, were his two customers. The photo made him look like someone using a typewriter as a portable computer to make a fashion statement or stand out.

As the Reddit community put it, he looked like a "fucking hipster":

Something about the picture filled anonymous Reddit commenters with rage:

"Fucking hipster piece of shit."

"I have never wanted to fist fight someone so badly in my entire life."

"Now swap your iPhone for a pigeon."

"So hipster it hurts."

"Just an attention whore with zero brains. Sorry to judge, but that's obviously what's the problem here."

"Some days, I really want to be a bully."

"Get the fuck out of my city."

Before CD woke up in the morning, his image had made it to Reddit's front page, where it was seen by hundreds of thousands of people. From there, other websites picked it up and mockingly posted it with captions like "Don't be this guy." Other sites promised visitors that the picture would make them "black out with rage."

CD did not enjoy seeing his business model taken out of context. Reading through the pages of personal attacks was a painful experience. He recalls:

> *"Of course I read every single comment. I did not ready myself mentally for a barrage of hipster-hating Internet commenters critiquing me for everything: my pale skin, my outfit, my hair, my typing style, my glasses. An entire sub-thread was devoted to whether or not I had shaved legs."*

Ultimately, CD decided to "out himself" in the Reddit thread and clarify that the photo was one of him conducting his Roving Typist business. Once a real person became attached to the "hipster" in the picture, people became a lot more polite in the Reddit thread. Some of the more harsh commenters deleted their previous statements; others gave him words of encouragement.

Still, as some commenters had threatened to smash the typewriter over his head, CD worried about going back out in public to type. "A typewriter is pretty heavy," CD jokes. "Smashing it on my head would probably kill me."

Nevertheless, CD continued going to the park and making good money from his stories. After posting on Reddit that he would be out typing, a bunch of friendly "Redditors" came out to see him. When people who worked at Reddit found out about his story, they invited him to the office to have a beer. His time as the most hated hipster in America was happily winding to a close.

Or so CD thought. Every few weeks, someone on the Internet would "discover" the picture and repost it with a snarky comment bashing hipsters. The low point came when CD's ex-girlfriend published an essay called "It happened to me: I got dumped by a meme" on a widely-read feminist blog.

Moving On

Eventually, CD learned to ignore the Internet comments. The anonymous commenters threatening to punch him never showed up at the High Line, and his customers remained satisfied with his stories.

Months later, CD found himself at a party with an editor from The Awl, a popular blog. After a few drinks, CD summoned up his liquid courage and pitched the editor his story of becoming a hipster meme. The editor was interested and agreed to publish the essay on his site and pay CD for it.

When CD published his essay, "I Am An Object Of Internet Ridicule, Ask Me Anything," in the fall of 2013, it went viral. His well-written defense didn't stop the original picture from continually making the Internet rounds – but it did arouse the interest of a documentarian, Mark Cersosima, who later chronicled CD's tale in a short film.

To CD and his artist friends, there was great irony to CD's story: he generated lots of free press, but it barely boosted business. Normally, media exposure leads to book sales, speaking engagements, or any of the accoutrements of fame. But in CD's case, it amounted to nothing. His fame wasn't associated with who he was; he was just an anonymous face on a picture on the web. Whenever it went re-viral, nothing happened for him and he certainly didn't make any money from it. People just wrote more mean things about him.

Around the time the short documentary launched, CD tried to come up with a way to benefit from his "fame" as the Roving Typist. With help from his old *Story and a Picture* friend Max, CD set up a website version of his business. For monetary donations, CD would write and send them custom stories. That way, CD figured, if people liked what they saw in the documentary, something positive might come from his Internet fame.

CD's gambit paid off: When the documentary launched, he got hundreds of orders! With donations ranging from $5 to $200 per story, CD had managed to salvage some financial success from his unexpected Internet fame. The online story request feature was so successful he had to temporarily disable new orders until he could fulfill his backlog.

Today, CD has graduated from his masters program, has a part-time job in publishing, and continues spending time as a roving typist. In fact, he's probably the most famous roving typist in the world. While that's a small distinction, it means that he occasionally gets hired by companies to provide his typing services at events. Large corporations have even hired him to give talks on creativity. His business is growing.

CD found a way to make the best of being called a "fucking hipster" and use it to help his business. His experience still makes him wonder: "Why did people on the Internet hate me so much just because of a picture in which I looked like a hipster?" In CD's view, this "hipster" hatred stems from a deep-seated rage that people feel against those who do not conform:

> *"There is a knee-jerk reaction to people who don't fit in or are intentionally doing the opposite. Why are they allowed to act abnormally when I have to work so hard to be normal?"*

CD says he's learned that you shouldn't make assumptions about why a stranger is doing something unusual, like using a typewriter in a park. Most people have reasonable, interesting explanations for why they're doing what they're doing. In CD's case, he didn't have a typewriter because he was desperate for attention – he was just a broke student trying to pay his way through school.

"There is a story behind everything," says CD, "you just have to ask."

ROBOT DANCE PARTY

Seven years ago at Burning Man, while wearing a homemade robot costume, Chris Hirst had a transcendental experience.

Through two small holes in a poster board-covered milk crate, he peered out at hundreds of grooving eccentrics. Criss-crossed straps dug into into his shoulders like piano wire; fifty pounds of plywood pressed violently on his collarbones. But none of this mattered to Chris. He had just sparked an extemporaneous dance revolution. Inside his speaker-equipped robot suit, he shuffle-stepped with the mechanical precision of a Singaporean pop singer.

When "Zoot Suit Riot" gave way to David Bowie's "As the World Falls Down," the crowd grew quiet and partnered up. Ensconced in the light of a full desert moon, the robot silently shed tears of joy.

The robot would have quite a journey in the coming years. He would become a San Francisco icon and a symbol of the uninhibited human spirit.

But first, he had to be rebuilt.

Birth and Early Robothood

Since its inception, Chris Hirst's robot has been a collaboration of minds. Huge clubs and music venues overwhelmed Chris and his friend Enzo, so they began toying with the idea of creating intimate, impromptu dance parties. Though "not a good dancer by any stretch of the imagination," Chris was piqued by the free-spirited nature of musical movement. Plus, he played a lot of Dance Dance Revolution, and that had to count for something.

The duo first tried fashioning a system of mini speakers into a business suit. This proved impractical, as the pant legs could not support the heavy equipment. They realized they'd need some sort of frame to house the speakers.

Then, Chris says, "the idea kind of just materialized – a robot!"

Enter the first roadblock: they knew absolutely nothing about wires, electronics, or, generally, how to construct anything at all.

Chris spent the summer of 2007 in the garage of his parents' suburban home, planning out schematics and constructing robot 1.0. The result was rudimentary. Thick plywood nailed into a rectangular box formed a "horrendous" internal support system that housed 12-pound speakers. For the bot's head, Chris covered a milk crate with silver-sprayed poster board; for the legs, he used flexible metal ducting. It was, by Chris's estimation, "an absolutely terrible design."

At this stage, Chris constructed the robot strictly for Burning Man purposes. Despite its shortcomings, Chris says robot 1.0 served its intended purpose at the event: "[The robot] provided the music, and danced worse than you would ever hope to. He set a nice, low bar that even closet dance enthusiasts could surpass."

People liked the robot, which inspired Chris to keep working on it. He enlisted the help of his friend Scott, who had a deeper knowledge of electronics, amps, and "assorted fake-robot-building skills." Over the following year, the two upgraded the speakers, rewired the amps, and added a motorcycle battery to power the rig.

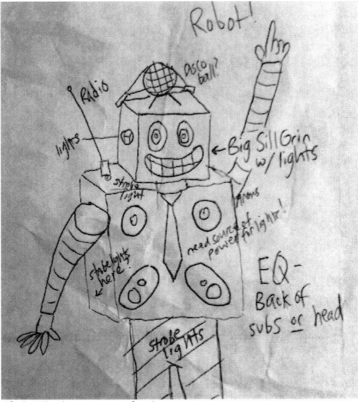

Chris Hirst's prototype dawing

They returned to Burning Man to great fanfare, but several serious problems still needed to be addressed.

For one thing, Chris could barely move in the unbearably heavy suit. "It was like dancing in a tank," he recalls. In preparation for Maker Faire, a popular DIY festival and showcase, he began putting together the final version of the robot — one that would be lighter, louder, and more danceable than its predecessors.

The resulting robot 3.0, also known as "Robot Dance Party," is the version admirers know and love today. Chris, now working alone, replaced the bot's unwieldy plywood frame with fiberglass and swapped the 12-pound speakers for 8-ounce speakers. He upgraded the painful support system to a pair of guitar straps and a belt-like mechanism that could be "slipped on like a shirt." He retooled the arms and legs with plastic AC ducting coated in mylar (the same material used to make space suits) and added clamp-like hands. Chris's 50-year-old neighbor, Dennis, even chipped in a few cooling fans for especially intense dance-offs.

Chris, who describes himself as "the kind of guy who buys the first pair of shoes [he tries] on," used measured simplicity in designing his alter-ego. He made it leaner, cleaner, and meaner.

The changes cut the robot's weight down to 25 pounds and made it look a hell of a lot better. Having gone through "robot puberty," the once-homely bot had matured into a suave silver fox. It was time for him to seek out greener pastures.

Dolores Park and the Loss of Innocence

Until this point, the robot had mainly provided family-friendly amusement for small children and entertained innocuous hippies rolling on molly. When Chris decided to debut the robot in Dolores Park, a popular San Francisco hang-out spot, things got physical. Though Chris deliberately made the robot androgynous and emotionally distant (it sports a permanent half-smirk), he says many park patrons have sexualized it:

> *"Girls love to come up and grind on the robot. I don't really understand it. It's definitely something that doesn't happen at Maker Faire."*

Though Chris has received an array of advice from his Dolores Park fans – "You should glue a giant rubber schlong on the robot, bro!" – he considers most of it in violation of the true spirit and purpose of his creation: to bring wholesome, random enjoyment into people's everyday lives, one dance at a time.

For a few admirers, the robot has conjured more than joy. Last year, one female fan relentlessly stalked the robot on Twitter, sharing his posts, favoriting every photo, and beckoning for a meet-up. Nearly every time he visits the park on a nice day, Chris says the robot is fondled, inappropriately touched, or molested. But Chris doesn't want to pigeonhole the robot as a sex symbol, so he often spends mornings in Helen Diller Playground performing for children, before migrating to the "pastures of passion" in the afternoon:

> *"Dancing for kids is more fun than dancing for adults. I think for adults, the robot is more of a novelty; kids just completely lose themselves in the dance. They love it. They don't hesitate to immediately join in on something spontaneous and silly. This one kid blew my mind last year with his dance moves – pure genius."*

Chris attributes this to the "suspension of disbelief" in which viewers, as poet Samuel Coleridge put it, brush over any implausibilities when you "infuse human interest and a semblance of truth" into something fantastical. Children are more apt to believe the robot is real, but Chris says he's seen plenty of adults debate whether or not there's a human inside.

"Dude, I wish I hadn't seen you take your head off," one bro in his twenties told Chris last year. "I had myself...believing you were real."

Robot Economics

Successful appearances in Dolores Park led to paying gigs. Soon, people recruited the robot to dance at their parties. Today, Robot Dance Party performs at three to five events per month. As he adjusts his fee based on clients' ability to pay, Chris's returns widely vary. A Sonoma winery once paid him $300 for a two-hour performance; the organizers of a 5k charity run paid in silly string.

The robot even has a quasi-manager, Mustafa Khan, who handles bookings and doubles as his occasional DJ. A former Facebook employee, Mustafa met the robot in Dolores Park and immediately saw potential. He helped the robot get off the ground, and he estimates that he's booked about 30 shows in the past year.

While Chris doesn't always agree with Mustafa's song choices (mostly highly recognizable, dance-friendly tunes like Hot Chocolate's "You Sexy Thing"), he admits he has a "weak spot for dancing to Katy Perry." But when he chooses the songs, Chris blasts Yo La Tengo, Pet Shop Boys, and Nine Inch Nails. His favorite song to boogie to? Billy Idol's Dancing With Myself.

Occasionally, Chris is offered corporate-sponsored gigs. Treasure Island Music Festival gave the robot free tickets, and ferried him out. He hasn't yet been hired for a bachelorette party, although Chris says he'll try anything once.

But creating a robot alter ego isn't cheap, and the monetary rewards are paltry in comparison to expenses. Chris estimates that he's invested $5,000 of his own money on parts, repairs, and batteries over the course of the robot's life. "Hot glue alone," he says, "has run me about $300." By day, Chris is an office manager at a software company, and in 2012, he decided he could no longer single-handedly fund his mylar-matted automaton. So, the robot turned to Kickstarter to help crowdfund his expenses.

In 30 days, the robot exceeded his goal, raising over $2,000 from 83 backers, mostly strangers who'd participated in his Dolores dance parties. The money helped Chris add glowing electroluminescent wires, arduino hardware that syncs the robot's lights to its music, and an interface that allows dancers to play their own music on his speakers from their mp3 players and phones. Most importantly, it funded new batteries, paint, and other maintenance items that keep the robot in party mode.

Dancing Into the Sunset

As a child, Chris Hirst took piano lessons. "Recitals were hell," he recalls, with a chuckle. "I remember walking out onto the stage, legs shaking, heart pounding. But the moment I played that first note, this calmness overtook me. It was like zen meditation. I was invisible."

Zen moments were rare for Chris growing up. He suffered from epilepsy and was diagnosed as bipolar at a young age. But today, the robot is his sanctum sanctorum, his escape, his "first note." Looking out from the solace of the robot, Chris sees a world full of energy, possibilities, and potential dance floors.

The robot, a reigning symbol of mindless, mechanical action, seems to instead conjure the true essence of the human spirit, inspiring creativity and spontaneity where he roams. When he makes an appearance, "people shed their insecurities and let themselves loose."

In many ways, Chris became his robot. Once reserved and self-conscious, he is now liberated and at peace. Even dressed in a blue button-up shirt and khakis, "Office Chris" walks with Robot Dance Party's jaunty step. In conversation, he often refers to himself as "the robot" subconsciously.

Robot Dance Party pleasing park-goers

But for all the enjoyment he's given to the community, Chris takes little credit and seeks no recognition.

"I'm not a person," he insists, "just music personified.

THE MAN WHO SMUGGLES TRADER JOE'S INTO CANADA

There is no Trader Joe's in Canada.

Imagine – maybe you don't have to – you're Canadian. You're at a dinner party, and the host has put out a bowl of snacks. It's the best snack you've ever had. Love at first bite, and it's going fast. Soon enough, your fingers graze the bottom of the bowl, and you realize that the end is nigh. You master your panic.

"Host," you chime. "Who makes these chocolate caramel peanut butter mango pretzel chip things?" You wait with bated breath and crumb-covered lips.

"Trader Joe's," he replies, and your heart shatters. This dinner party is in Vancouver. A trip to the nearest Trader Joe's in Bellingham, Washington, takes hours, including additional hours spent crossing the border and in the crowded store. Just thinking about it causes the snack, once so sweet and savory, to turn acrid on your tongue.

Your host notices your grimace and chuckles. "Chill dude," he says, with smiling eyes. "I bought these in Vancouver. You can too."

Your mind wrestles with the information. "There's a Trader Joe's in Vancouver now?"

"No, there's a Pirate Joe's in Vancouver."

A Pirate's Life

Michael Hallatt is an itinerant adventurer and a man of many trades. Lithe and grey-eyed, kind and intense, he speaks quickly – leaping from story to joke to political opinion and onto the next revolution, woe betide those who can't keep up. He's worked as a designer, a baker, a programmer, a carpenter, a filmmaker and – for the past two and a half years – a "pirate" who imports Trader Joe's foods across the US-Canadian border.

Hallatt first developed his taste for Trader Joe's back in 2000. He worked for AskJeeves, a once-popular, pre-Google search engine, and lived in Mill Valley, a "food snob" town in the San Francisco suburbs just outside Trader Joe's territory. But when the Internet Bubble burst, he got out of software and bought a fixer-upper house in Emeryville, a blue-collar town east of San Francisco.

"I was living on the construction site and pinching pennies," he tells us. "I'd go to the nearby Trader Joe's and fill up a shopping cart with frozen tamales and enchiladas. I lived off that."

"I ended up falling in love with someone, and our daughter was basically conceived on tamales." His partner was from Vancouver, so they eventually left the house Hallatt built – now a striking, spacious two-story he called "the Buddhahouse" – and moved back to his native Canada.

"All of a sudden my life was in a place where I needed a day job," Hallatt says. "I knew that probably meant being a middle manager at a software company, and I'd done that already."

He adds, "Or I had to start something!" He found himself reminiscing about his pre-software career, and the bagelry he dropped out of design school to open in the 1980s. He also found himself "jonesing for some TJ's," so he made the trek to Bellingham.

"The place was full of Canadians," Hallatt says, "and I'm a bit of a stranger talker." In the checkout line, he groused with the other Canadians about coming all this way to get their Trader Joe's fix. Somebody mentioned a lady in Point Roberts, an American city that is contiguous with mainland Canada, who set up a home delivery service for a limited number of Trader Joe's items. This got Hallatt thinking.

By the time he got to the register, Hallatt had conceived the idea for Pirate Joe's. He would buy large quantities of Trader Joe's products in the U.S. and import them to Canada. Very large quantities – enough to stock a physical store. He'd make regular border runs to keep the inventory fresh, and mark up the products to cover rent and operations. Voila! Canadians would get their Trader Joe's products without the trek, Trader Joe's would get a "presence" in Canada without the legal hassle, and Hallatt would get to be his own boss at a fun and funky "day job."

During the trip, Hallatt also met "Kyle," who introduced himself as the manager of the Bellingham store. Kyle agreed to help him out, because supplying Hallatt would be a huge boon for the Bellingham store's sales.

"It took us six months to figure the whole thing out," Hallatt says.

For one thing, he needed a storefront. He bought a space that was previously a Romanian Bakery and fixed up the roof and left up the sign. "It was clunky, but a great find on the outside," he says. "It looked like the funkiest coolest weirdo from another age. Who was I to tear it down? It was a tribute to the soul of the place." 'Transylvania Peasant Bread' became 'Transylvania Trading Company' – which was to be his store's first front.

Hallatt wanted to import his stock legally. Thanks to the North American Free Trade Agreement, Hallatt could transport most of his goods duty-free, but he had so much to declare that he wrote a computer program to generate a barcode to summarize his haul. "Of course, the system broke right away," Hallatt says. The barcode wouldn't scan. "I was stuck at the border, with a trailer, in the winter, on a shoestring."

In order to sell the items in Canada, he also had to print out new nutrition labels for each of them that met Canadian regulations. He devised a system, then drove to Bellingham and bought one of everything to test it. "The cashiers co-operated. They knew what I was doing, so it was an easy checkout – instead of going through the cart, they just charged me for one of everything."

Hallatt took a lot more trips to Bellingham in those six months. Every time, Kyle would be at the store, waiting for him and egging him on.

"At some point I asked, 'What if corporate finds out?'" Hallatt says. "And Kyle said, 'They're too stoned to find out.'"

The first full haul was seamless, and the Transylvania Trading Company successfully opened its doors on January 1, 2012. The store welcomed a slow trickle of confused customers – some of whom loved the store once they discovered its offerings. But during the second haul, Hallatt discovered that Kyle was the junior manager of the store, not the head honcho running the location. Kyle's boss – the Bellingham store's senior manager – came out to ask a few questions. The senior manager called corporate for guidance, which is how, his second week in business, Hallatt was banned from his first Trader Joe's.

"So I just started buying stuff out of Seattle," he says, nonchalantly. "There's more stores and more selection there anyways."

Trader Joe's sent Hallatt a cease and desist letter; he put it up in the window and carried on. Business proceeded pretty quietly for a while. Pricing took some time to figure out. (Today, it's still not an exact science: Hallatt marks up the "luxury" items more to subsidize the basics.) The store relocated to another address in Vancouver. New clientele heard about the store by word-of-mouth, and staff instructed customers to keep the operation on the down-low.

Occasionally a journalist would write about the store and cause a minor uproar. One journalist nicknamed the store "Pirate Joe's." It stuck, and according to Hallatt, "it ended up being convenient shorthand for our tagline: 'unauthorized, unaffiliated, and unafraid.'" Hallatt hired shoppers across the border to help him with runs – he learned he couldn't hire Canadians to do it without a work visa. Sometimes specific shoppers got banned from specific stores, which just meant they had to rotate to a new beat.

This went on for about a year and a half. Then, in May of 2013, Trader Joe's sued Michael Hallatt.

The Grey Area of the Grey Market

Back when Hallatt formed the idea for Pirate Joe's, many people told him, "You're gonna get sued." He heard it from everyone – from friends who hysterically shouted, "This is absolutely insane!" to friends who suggested, "Ah, dude, why don't you just find something else to do?"

But Hallatt was determined, so he did his research. One term that kept turning up was "grey market."

Pirate Joe's isn't technically engaging in piracy. The stock isn't stolen (Hallatt pays retail to Trader Joe's for all his stock), counterfeit (Hallatt's products are advertised as Trader Joe's products, and are in fact Trader Joe's products), or even technically smuggled (Hallatt declares his haul at customs, and he doesn't stock alcohol, which is highly regulated). Pirate Joe's deals in a grey market, i.e. trading products outside of their official, authorized distribution channels. Authorized goods are white market; illegal goods are black market. Grey market goods are somewhere in between.

A classic example of a grey market is the online retail of electronics equipment. Suppliers will set different prices for the same product in different regions, but an online customer can opt to import a product from a cheaper region if he or she chooses. One online retailer, for example, sells the same Nikon lens for $839 as a grey market import and $899 from the official American distributor. The retailer provides free, expedited shipping for both items.

Many respectable retailers openly sell products acquired through "unofficial" channels without incurring the legal wrath of their suppliers. Hallatt even discovered that Joe Coulombe – the original owner and CEO of Trader Joe's, which is now controlled by the German owners of a discount supermarket chain – defended his decision to sell grey market stock in the 1980's. According to a 1988 article in the Los Angeles Times, Trader Joe's sold bottles of Dom Perignon for $33 a pop – about half its price at many other stores:

> *"'It was stupid to buy from official sources,' said Joe Coulombe, chairman of Trader Joe's, which used to buy all its French champagne from gray market sources. 'We sold millions of dollars of stuff.'"*

Hallatt says he still has a lot of respect for Trader Joe's and "what they're trying to do with food." He says he runs the store out of love for the label and cites Coulombe's example as a reason he persevered through the lawsuit.

Hallatt also learned that a lot of grey market entrepreneurs battled regulation and won. One college student had his friends in Asia send him copies of textbooks, which he then resold to an American clientele on eBay, netting an estimated $100,000 in profit. The textbook publisher took him to court, and the student fought back, claiming he was protected by an aspect of U.S. copyright law called the "first sale doctrine." The first sale doctrine basically says that once you've bought something, it's yours and you can do what you want with it.

The case made it to the Supreme Court, which ruled in the student's favor. From Justice Breyer's reading of the court opinion:

> *"We ask whether the 'first sale' doctrine applies to protect a buyer or other lawful owner of a copy [...] lawfully manufactured abroad. Can that buyer bring that copy into the United States (and sell or give it away) without obtaining permission to do so from the copyright owner? Can [...] someone who purchases [...] a book printed abroad subsequently resell it without the copyright owner's permission? In our view, the answers to these questions are, yes."*

The decision came just months before Trader Joe's sued Hallatt.

Pirate versus Goliath

Once he knew where to look, Hallatt called lawyers who specialized in grey market law for a free consult. The lawyers found that Trader Joe's had a history of suing people for infringing on their trademark.

But some lawyers encouraged him to pursue his idea, even ones who knew about Trader Joe's legal history. "One guy said," Hallatt reports, dropping his voice to a whisper to quote the attorney, "'You can totally do this. I normally crush guys like you, but you can totally do this.'"

Another pair of lawyers argued about the case until they came to an impasse. "There were a few beats of silence," Hallatt says, "and then one of them said, 'You should take fact that we can't say "no" as a really good sign.'"

"But then they wanted a retainer to stay on and keep me from getting sued, and I didn't have the money for that!" Hallatt laughs.

When he did get slapped with a lawsuit, he "thanked God" he had valid business insurance, which is how he's afforded his legal fees.

In late 2013, the case was dismissed with prejudice – Hallatt won. Trader Joe's is appealing.

The biggest issue with the lawsuit was that Pirate Joe's is in Canada, and Trader Joe's and its lawsuit were not. This was the exact language in the case:

> *"Plaintiff does not state a claim upon which relief can be granted because [Washington laws] do not apply where no Party is a Washington resident, all allegedly wrongful conduct occurs out of state, and any harm to Washington residents is extremely tangential if existent."*

This leaves Hallatt in a kind of reverse catch-22: either way, he wins. The court says Trader Joe's doesn't have a claim if they don't have a presence in Canada. If Trader Joe's ever opens a Canadian store, they might have a claim. But Hallatt's ultimate goal with Pirate Joe's is to "bring" Trader Joe's to Canada. Before he had the store, he would call Trader Joe's and petition the company to open a Canadian store, and Hallat has always promised to close up shop if Trader Joe's ever expands north. In many ways, Hallatt would count this as the ultimate victory. "I'd take a little backhanded credit for it," he jokes, "and move onto the next thing."

The case attracted a lot of media attention and speculation by legal experts in a few popular outlets. Some of them, along with Hallatt's lawyers, pointed out that the case would be shaky even if it weren't straddling a national border. Law Professors Kal Raustiala and Chris Sprigman noted:

> *"Trademark law doesn't confer on trademark owners the right to control subsequent unauthorized resales of genuine products, at least if the reseller doesn't alter the product in a way that confuses consumers. [Pirate Joe's] doesn't do anything to the [Trader Joe's] products other than truck them across the border in a white panel van.*
>
> *If [Trader Joe's] has the right to stop [Pirate Joe's] from reselling their products, then any trademark owner might assert a similar right. Ford could sue Carmax for reselling Fords. [...] And if this were true, a trademark law that is aimed at preventing consumer confusion will be preventing something else entirely – competition."*

Business as Usual

If you call Pirate Joe's during off-hours, or while the staff are too busy to answer the phone, you'll hear Hallatt's scratchy voice on the recording:

> *"Hi you've reached Pirate Joe's we're located at 2348 West 4th Street [...]*

We do not sell Trader Joe's products. You might have heard we do, we don't. That would be unfair to Trader Joe's, to go down there and buy groceries from them. Say you bought like maybe a million dollars worth of groceries from them over three years, that would be grossly unfair, paid cash. Terrible terrible. So, you know, we don't. We didn't do that...

HA!

Come on down, check out what we got. Or call us back, bug us, we'll pick up we'll tell you what we've have. Mostly costumes [unintelligible]."

This is Hallatt kidding around. But he's also playing up his store's surreal aesthetic. Hallatt says he loves new customers who show up visibly uneasy.

"There's a hesitation like, 'Am I going to get arrested?'" Hallatt says. It helps if there are a lot of empty spaces on the shelves. "Maybe somebody came and took all the damn mangoes or something. And we say, 'We've got someone shopping right now. It'll be back in a few days.'"

Hallatt seems to relish how the sloppiness of his store disrupts the normal, transactional culture of buying groceries. "You usually walk into a grocery store thinking 'OK I gotta get my stuff and get going, I've got two quarters in the meter.'"

But Pirate Joe's is a dangerous place to come into.

"We try to give them a basket, and they know what that means. If they grab a basket, they're in trouble. So then we offer them chocolate." Hallatt laughs. "The chocolate is usually a pretty effective icebreaker." While eating chocolate, customers are comfortable enough to ask questions, so Hallatt tells them his story.

Michael Hallett: the captain of Pirate Joes

In July of 2014, "docu-reality comedy" Nathan for You made a splash by opening a "parody" Starbucks. They claimed they could use Starbucks' trademarks because their store wasn't really a store; it was a piece of performance art. If the appeal goes south for Hallatt, his lawyers might want to try this tactic. He's in it for the adventure, the romance, the ideals, and the drama, which isn't something every small business owner can say.

Even a pirate's life has its lulls. "It's so boring right now. I'm craving something," Hallatt tells us when we ask him about business. He's eyeing a second location, farther from the border. The shipments come in steadily enough. He's got eight or so shoppers working right now, spending a couple thousand dollars a week. He still does border crossings himself, sitting in line for hours in an unmarked white van. The workload is enormous. Hallatt jokes that whenever a cab goes by, he envies the driver's salary.

A few years back, Hallatt's old software friends invited him to work with them as a developer for Wells Fargo. He could probably get back into development if he wanted, but his heart belongs to the store.

Part of his fidelity to the place is political. He says that even with the "pirate" markup, his products are often a better deal than those found at the Safeway across the street, and for that to be the case, there must be something wrong with the Canadian economy.

The store has also become a minor tourist site. The whole lawsuit was a bath in the limelight for Hallatt. He was interviewed for newspapers and radio, and he made a few television appearances. ("I made Fox News send a limo because I hate Murdoch.") Kids from the Sauder School of Business come by every once in a while to check the place out and do a case study. ("I tell them it isn't a business model – it's a stunt!") People come from all over just to see his store. One guy, from the "outer reaches," came to the store just to shake Hallatt's hand. He told Hallatt he was proud of him.

"How do you quit when you have that kind of encouragement?" Hallatt pleads. "I end up having to suspend my own rational thinking. I've never worked harder for less money in my life."

THE INVENTION OF
THE AEROPRESS

For coffee aficionados, the AeroPress is a revelation. A small, $30, plastic device that resembles a plunger, it makes what many consider to be the best cup o' Joe in the world. Proponents of the AeroPress claim that its coffee is tastier than that produced by thousand-dollar machines and expert-level baristas; it even seems to magically clean itself with every use.

There's really nothing bad to say about the Aero-Press other than that it's a funny-looking plastic thingy. Then again, its inventor, Stanford professor Alan Adler, is a world-renowned inventor of funny-looking plastic thingies. While Adler's Palo Alto-based company, Aerobie, is best-known today for its coffee makers, the firm rose to prominence in the 1980s for its world-record-setting flying discs.

Over a period of nearly three decades, Adler and Aerobie defied the notion of industry-specific limitations and found immense success in two disparate industries: toys and coffee.

The Rise of Aerobie

In 1938, a man named Fred Morrison was out on Santa Monica Beach with his wife when he found a pie tin. The two began tossing it back and forth, and another beachgoer approached Morrison and offered him 25 cents for the tin – five times its retail price in stores.

Morrison saw potential for a market.

Upon returning from World War II, he designed an aerodynamically improved plastic disc and sold it at trade shows as the "Flyin-Saucer." After being accused of using invisible wire to make his discs hover, he developed a killer sales pitch: "The Flyin-Saucer is free, but the invisible wire is $1." He made about $2 million off his invention, then sold it to toy company Wham-O in 1957. Wham-O renamed the product the "Frisbee."

Enter Edward "Steady Ed" Headrick, the modern Frisbee's founding father. Hedrick reworked the Frisbee's rim thickness and reshaped the top, making it more aerodynamic and easier to control. By forming leagues and tournaments, he also propelled the Frisbee into mainstream popularity. A true man of his craft, he requested his ashes be molded into memorial Frisbees and given to family and close friends upon his death – a request that was fulfilled when he passed in 2002.

After Headrick's modifications, the Frisbee went largely unchanged for many years. Then, Alan Adler came along.

***

Throughout the 1960s, Adler worked as an engineer in the private sector, designing things that the average person rarely sees: the controls to submarines and nuclear reactors, instrumentation systems for military aircraft, and a variety of optics. He also mentored engineering students at Stanford University, where he taught a course on sensors. "I was never happier than when I was learning a new discipline," he tells us.

This sense of curiosity led him to pursue a diverse range of hobbies, and as "the type of person who always seeks ways to make things better," his hobbies invariably led to inventions. Today, he owns over 40 patents – some of which are in surprising fields.

As an amateur astronomer in the early 2000s, Adler invented a new type of paraboloid mirror and wrote a computer program, Sec, that assisted astronomers in selecting secondary mirrors. He developed an interest in sailing and proceeded to design a sailboat that won the heralded Transpac race from San Francisco to Hawaii. Shortly after taking up the Shakuhachi, a traditional Japanese end-blown flute, he proceeded to build his own from PVC pipe and metal.

Adler had always been particularly fascinated by the magical quality of flight, which drew on his engineering skills and appealed to his free spirit. So in the mid-1970s, he began toying with the idea of creating a flying disc – an object that would be "easy for the average person to throw with very little effort." Eight years and dozens of prototypes later, the Skyro was born.

The Skyro relied on a basic principle of aerodynamics: a flying ring requires an equal amount of lift in the back and the front. Unfortunately, the back end of a flying ring always caught the downdraft of the front, which prevented a stable, balanced flight. To combat this, Adler fine tuned the molding of the Skyro to create an "extremely low-drag shape."

Adler took his design to Parker Brothers, a toy manufacturer, met with one of their sales managers, and "went out in the parking lot to throw discs around for a while." The manager was blown away by the disc's ease of flight, but it was made out of rigid plastic and he insisted it was too hard for recreational use. In his design, Adler included instructions to line the edges with soft rubber during the manufacturing process, but it required pioneering a new technique that Parker Brothers deemed "impossible."

"They didn't have the foresight to do something that hadn't been done," Adler tells us. So, in typical Alder fashion, he did it himself. He went to Mother Lode Plastics, paid them "several thousand dollars," and had custom molds made for a prototype. He then brought his completed vision, now with soft rubber edges, back to Parker Brothers, and they bought the rights to his invention.

Under Parker Brothers' control, the Skyro sold about a million units – not quite enough to "maintain the company's interest," according to Adler. In the early 1980s, he purchased back the rights to his invention.

The Skyro had one major issue: it had to be thrown at a very particular speed in order for it to fly in a straight trajectory. When it was thrown at the right speed, it flew insane distances – from home plate, one man threw a Skyro out of Dodger Stadium. But for the average consumer, it could be difficult to determine this speed. Adler went back to the drawing board.

**

Over six long years, Adler taught classes and worked as a consultant by day and developed the ultimate flying disc at night. In January of 1984, while using a ring-flight computer simulator he designed, Adler realized that achieving a perfect balance at any speed was possible. To achieve this, he'd have to create an airfoil (a wing or blade) around the perimeter of the disc that allowed for "50% greater lift slope when flying forward than backward."

On his fourth prototype, Adler had a major breakthrough: he molded a "spoiler" lip around the outside of the rim, which acted as an airfoil. When he took his new model out to a big field on Stanford's campus and thrust it into the air, the disc flew "as if sliding on an invisible sheet of ice."

"The first time I threw the Aerobie, I was in a state of euphoria," Adler recalls. "It made such an impact on me. It went so far with such little effort."

Within six months, Adler's first disc, The Aerobie Pro, went into independent production under Adler's new company, Superflight, Inc (known today as Aerobie, Inc). Adler recalls the thrill of releasing his invention:

> *"For years, in my consulting work, I worked on things the average person wouldn't buy. It was a great pleasure to transition into products with much broader utility and distribution. Plus, Aerobies are a whole lot of fun. When you see a beautiful flight, it elevates your whole soul."*

The Aerobie flying ring's story – zany college engineering professor invents incredible flying toy – made for a good headline. Adler says this led to a "fabulous run of luck with publicity," which led to the product's early success:

> *"We were on all of the networks: The New York Times, People Magazine – just about all the major news sources we wanted covered us. Stanford's news service sent out 220 press releases about the disc."*

Adler also got creative with marketing. He contacted Scott Zimmerman, a seven-time Frisbee World Champion, and involved him in a number of publicity stunts through the mid-1980s. In 1986, Zimmerman threw an Aerobie Pro 1,257 feet (383.1 meters) at Fort Funston, San Francisco, setting a Guinness World Record for "longest throw of an object without any velocity-aiding feature." In 1987, Zimmerman dressed in full George Washington regalia, taped a silver dollar to an Aerobie, and hurled it across the Potomac River.

In 1988, he flung an Aerobie over Niagara Falls.

Adler offered a $1,000 reward to whoever could break the Guinness record set by Zimmerman. In 2003, Erin Hemmings threw the disc 1,333 feet – over a quarter of a mile – and collected the money. His record-breaking throw was in the air for "more than 30 seconds."

Alan Adler, with an early prototype of the Aerobie Pro

By 1986 – two years into production – the Aerobie Pro had sold one million units in the United States and another 400,000 abroad in Canada, the U.K., and Germany. Adler became a "folk hero" on the Stanford campus; the school's bookstore sold 6,680 Aerobies in only a 10 month period – one for every two students. At the time, Adler had a goal: to beat the Frisbee's all-time sales of 10 million units. Today, he's getting pretty close.

While the flying ring has been Aerobie's best-selling toy product, the company has released an array of other aerodynamically sound toys – eighteen, to be exact – ranging from a football with fins to the Dogobie, a "dog-proof" disc.

Aerobie has also undergone a transition from selling to toy retailers to selling to sporting good stores, according to Aerobie's business manager, Alex Tennant:

> *"When I came to work here twenty years ago, our largest segment of customers was toy stores; now 80+% of our sales are to sporting goods retailers. Our products sell year after year in sporting goods stores whereas toy stores and toy departments tend to feel that they must sell whatever is new."*

The toy industry has a tendency to push out new products every three years, clarifies Adler, and big manufacturers like Parker Brothers often enforce quotas of up to ten new toys every year. Aerobie finds this practice counterintuitive.

Aerobie has stuck with a relatively small list of 18 products over its 30 years in business, and it has never had to discontinue a product, which is a routine practice for major toy manufacturers.

Yet despite the Aerobie Pro's incredible popularity, the AeroPress coffee maker has replaced it as the company's all-time best-seller.

How Aerobie Disrupted the Coffee Game

Alan Adler conceived the AeroPress at his dinner table. The company was having a team meal, when the wife of Aerobie's sales manager asked, "What do you guys do when you just want one cup of coffee?"

A long-time coffee enthusiast and self-proclaimed "one cup kinda guy," Adler had wondered this many times himself. He'd grown frustrated with his coffee maker, which yielded six to eight cups per brew. In typical Adler fashion, he didn't let the problem bother him long: he set out to invent a better way to brew a single cup of coffee.

First, he experimented with existing brewing methods. Automatic drip coffee makers were the most popular, but "coffee connoisseurs" seemed to prefer the pour-over method involving a filter in a ceramic cone, or the French Press. Adler quickly found the faults of each device.

The pour-over method, for example, involves lining a ceramic cone with a filter, filling it with grounds, and pouring hot water over them. The grounds infuse the water, which is then funneled through a hole in the bottom of the cone into a cup. But the longer the water mingles with the grounds (called the "wet time"), the more acidity and bitterness leaches into the drink. Adler says the pour-over method has "an average wet time of four to five minutes." Other common methods like the French Press and the automatic drip take more or less as long. Adler figured he could prevent bad-tasting byproducts by reducing this wet time.

It struck Adler that he could use air pressure to shorten this process. After a few weeks in his garage, he created a prototype: a plastic tube that used plunger-like action to compress the flavors quickly out of the grounds. He brewed his first cup with the invention and knew he'd made something special. Immediately, he called his business manager Alex Tennant.

Tennant tasted the brew and stepped back. "Alan," he said, "I can sell a ton of these."

Adler spent the next year perfecting the design, trying out different sizes and configurations. The final product, which he called the AeroPress, was simple to operate: you place a filter and two to four scoops of coffee grounds into a plastic tube, pour hot water into the tube at an optimal temperature of between 165 and 175 degrees, and stir for ten seconds.

Next comes the fun part: you insert the "plunger" into the tube and slowly press down. The air pressure forces the water through the grounds and into your coffee mug that is (hopefully) positioned below. This produces "pure coffee" that is close to espresso in strength and can be diluted with additional water. The process of plunging the tube also cleans the device, but Adler says this was simply "serendipitous." After all, he says, great inventions "always require a little luck."

The AeroPress in action

Adler's new method shortened the wet time from four to five minutes to one minute. Adler also touts that his paper filters, which run $3.50 for 350, are reusable up to 25 times each and reduce lipids that typically incite the body to produce LDL cholesterol – though these claims are hotly debated in the coffee community.

With his plans mapped out, Adler went to Westec Plastics in Livermore, California, ordered $100,000 worth of molds, and put the invention into production. In 2005, Tennant and Adler debuted the product at Seattle's Coffee Fest, where it was "extremely well accepted by the coffee aficionado community." Brewers loved the easily "hackable" design of the AeroPress; its list price of $29.99 didn't hurt either, especially when gauged against coffee makers ten to fifteen times the cost.

Despite a great showing, the AeroPress wasn't an instant hit with shoppers. The next few years were a struggle for Adler and his team. At one point, 2007 sales were lower than 2006 sales, and it looked like the product would fizzle out. After years of familiarizing himself with the sporting goods market, Tennant had to convince houseware distributors and retailers to sell "an odd looking, completely new kind of coffee maker made by a toy manufacturer."

When the AeroPress hit the market, the competition was formidable. "If you had walked down the coffee maker aisle at Target, you would have found many 8 to 12 cup drip coffee makers that sold for $20 to $50," says Tennant. But the AeroPress distinguished itself as part of a new trend towards one-cup brewing based on the idea that "fresher coffee is better coffee." And the AeroPress did brew a mean cup of joe.

The Aerobie team kept attending trade shows and sent out free products to coffee experts and food writers. In 2008, sales began to pick up. Aerobie had faith in the superiority of the AeroPress and, eventually, others did too. "There is no question," reiterates Tennant, "that the performance of the AeroPress and the delicious taste of the coffee it brews is the fundamental reason our strategy works."

The coffee community is rather fanatical; one popular forum, CoffeeGeek, boasts 82,000 members who debate everything from water dilution ratios to methods for doodling designs in the foamed milk at the top of a latte. The largest thread on the entire forum is "Aerobie AeroPress." It was created in 2005 and has accumulated over 7.3 million views and 2,700 posts. Adler joined the site, led discussions, and answered over 600 customer questions directly on the site.

Whereas Adler relied on traditional media and television to market his flying discs, the Internet brought the AeroPress great success – especially internationally. Interested customers contacted the company from all over the world, Adler recalls:

> *"You would not believe the coffee shop owners in remote corners of the world who contact us and ask how they can buy some AeroPress coffee makers. I guess the message is those corners are no longer so remote with the Internet."*

The World AeroPress Championship started at the behest of a Norwegian brewer who loved the product. Competitors use the AeroPress to brew the best cup of coffee, which is judged using a blind taste test. The World AeroPress Championship has attracted competitors from 25 countries and has helped boost international sales to 38% of Aerobie's overall revenue. The AeroPress has seen especially strong sales in Norway, Sweden, Denmark, and Finland, where people "are very serious about their coffee." The product is now sold in 56 countries worldwide.

Today, the AeroPress is Aerobie's best-selling and fastest-growing product; it accounts for nearly half of all the company's sales. Since 2005, Aerobie has sold over one million units and Tennant says the product is still gaining traction.

The AeroPress's "hackable" nature has led to a variety of barista-made supplementary inventions. In 2012, Seattle-based Keffeologie invented the S-Filter, a reusable metal filter for the AeroPress, and raised over $30,000 on Kickstarter with only a $500 initial goal. Portland-based Able Brewing Equipment invented a small stopper to convert the AeroPress into an on-the-go cup. Numerous companies have also made specialized brew stations for the device.

Coffee pros also heatedly debate whether brewing with the Aeropress upside down (inverted) results in superior taste. Some claim that the inverted method results in "total immersion brewing" like that of a French Press; others say the method is just a fancy way for baristas to distinguish themselves. Adler doesn't think the inverted method makes any difference in taste, and he says "about half" the winners of the AeroPress World Championships do it this way, and the other half don't. "Honestly," he admits, "I don't know if it's effective or not."

Adler's Reflections on Inventing

Alan Adler's two-car garage in Los Altos, California, isn't much good for parking.

"There's no way you can get a car in there," says Tennant. "It's just not going to happen." Two large industrial tools – a lathe and a milling machine – take up most of the space; boxes of prototypes, plastic molds, and relics of foregone creations pack every other conceivable nook and cranny. In here, says Adler, "the inventions are born."

A few times a year, Adler packs a small book bag and heads to his local junior high school to teach students about what he's learned in his garage over the years. Most of his students have no idea who he is, but they have probably tossed around an Aerobie Pro.

Adler imparts five of his inventing tips to his class:

1. *Learn all you can about the science behind your invention.*

2. *Scrupulously study the existing state of your idea by looking at current products and patents.*

3. *Be willing to try things even if you aren't too confident they'll work. Sometimes you'll get lucky.*

4. *Try to be objective about the value of your invention. People get carried away with the thrill of inventing and waste good money pursuing something that doesn't work any better than what's already out there.*

5. *You don't need a patent in order to sell an invention. A patent is not a business license; it's a permission to be the sole maker of a product (and even this is limited to 20 years).*

But Adler possesses a skill that can't be taught: tenacity. In the face of failure, he persists with a level head. Neither the Aerobie Pro, the AeroPress, nor any of his other 17 inventions came easily. But as Adler says, "inventing is a disease and there is no known cure."

***

As he digs through a box of his old prototypes in the Stanford Special Collections Library, Adler can't help but smile. "I haven't seen these in twenty years," he tells us, running a finger across his pencil-thin mustache. For nearly an hour, he examines his old toys, pausing to tell us the stories behind each – quite loudly, to the library staff's displeasure. With lit eyes, he watches a video reel of old Aerobie news spots: early 1980s Alan is animated, enthusiastic, full of life and vibrancy.

Before he leaves, Adler pulls aside a Stanford library employee. "I'm Alan Adler, inventor of the Aerobie," he tells the kid. "I'd like to donate my notebooks when I die; is that something I should handle through you?" The employee, no more than 20 years old, seems a bit taken aback, but sits down with Adler and discusses what the notebooks contain: decades of designs, equations, graphs, musings, and ideas – a treasure trove of ingenuity.

But the notebooks also contain years of failure, frustration, and miscalculation. At every turn, the AeroPress – like most of Adler's other inventions – encountered innumerable roadblocks. In many ways, the AeroPress is a reflection of its inventor: it's simple, but precise, highly adaptable, and squeezes every last drop of flavor from the bean.

THE MAN WHO SEES
ART IN CHEETOS

By day, Andy Huot is a mechanical engineer who designs "the equipment used to build aircraft parts." He's an intelligent man who choose his words wisely and provides straightforward answers. Goal-oriented and focused, he is rarely derailed by distractions. By night, he creates art with Cheetos.

Over the past year, the Louisville, Kentucky, resident has spent hours dipping his hands into greasy bags, examining each puffed corn nugget with the shrewd intensity of a museum curator, and posting his unaltered findings on photo-sharing site Instagram. Today, he has more than 40,000 followers from around the world.

It's been an unlikely journey for Huot – a journey of cheese-encrusted fingers, humor, and artistic discovery – and it all began with a Sasquatch-shaped Cheeto.

***

Last October, while working on an engineering-related invention at home, Huot got hungry. He didn't want to stop and make himself anything to eat. He wanted something quick, something he could munch on while tinkering.

"I'd bought some grocery store brand cheese curls, and I just started eating them," he tells us. "My creative mind was going at the time, and I was...I was able to see shapes in the Cheetos." Amused, he whipped out his phone and took a dozen photos of various humanoid cheese curls. When he showed them to his friends and family members, they were thoroughly amused. I wonder what I can do with this? he asked himself.

His little brother had an answer. "Dude," he said, "Instagram."

With his brother's help, Huot created Cheese Curls of Instagram, an account entirely composed of "pictures of Cheetos that resemble things." Expecting a minimal to non-existent response, he posted his first photo – Sasquatch:

Huot's first big Instagram hit: Sasquatch Cheeto

The torrent of support was like nothing he had ever experienced. Within hours, the Sasquatch Cheeto "blew up": dozens of people left words of high praise, "likes" poured in, and Huot accrued followers at a rate of 150 per day – "all organically," he says.

"I didn't expect that response," he admits. "It motivated me to keep going, to try harder."

Over the ensuing three months, Huot posted 40 more images, each escalating in both popularity and complexity. Whereas his early Cheeto visions were simple finds like a cat, hammerhead shark, and the number seven, he began to take bigger risks. One Cheeto titled Interpreter and Guide for The Lewis and Clark Expedition, Sacagawea, Nods Her Head as She Holds Her Baby, Jean Baptiste Charbonneau, for example, found an appreciative audience.

By the end of 2013, Huot had amassed a considerable and devout following. "You've inspired me," wrote one fan, "seriously – this is the most unique and epic page on Instagram." A more emphatic supporter wrote, "You're a fucking visionary."

Huot's success didn't come without criticism. Many commenters disliked his "un-manicured" fingernails and "cheesy fingers." In January, he began using tweezers to hold up his treats instead. But Huot, an ever-crafty engineer, wasn't satisfied, so he pioneered what is perhaps the most complex photography rig ever used to photograph a Cheeto. As he explains:

> *"I took a steel frame workbench with a wooden top, and bolted a drill press to it. On the plate, I clamped a tripod, which supports the camera. I can raise and lower the camera by cranking the drill press up and down, and I can swivel it at whatever angle I need.*
>
> *Then, I have this picture frame – a long, skinny picture frame with non-glare glass – protruding from the table like a diving board. That's where the Cheetos go. Underneath the glass, on the floor, I draped this bed sheet, you know – to give it some texture."*

Huot set up the rig in his son's room, where the natural light hit the Cheetos just right.

Even with the elaborate set-up, Huot encountered issues. "When I started taking the high quality pictures, there were two reflection problems," he says. "The camera seeing itself, and the Cheeto reflecting its orange light off the glass – like a halo."

To reduce glare, Huot enlisted a "circular polarizing filter" and wrapped his camera in a towel. The Cheetos' luminous glare was no more.

"The things I've had to do to get these Cheetos to look like they're floating," he admits, "are pretty crazy."

**

Curating Cheetos has slowly eaten up Huot's free time. He only spends 5 to 10 minutes in the morning and 20 minutes at night on Instagram, but his process of discovery is more time consuming.

Huot typically works an extra 30 minutes Monday through Thursday to allow himself a half-day every Friday – time he uses to sift through Cheetos. "First of all, I have to be eating them," Huot clarifies. "I can't just open a bag and look for good ones. It just doesn't work."

He'll pop open a bag and remove each cheesy nugget, slowly examining it "from all angles." If he deems one visually unstimulating, he eats it.

When Huot first began, he exclusively ate jalapeno-cheddar Cheetos. But after eating a bag a week for a few months, he grew weary of the flavor and switched to "flaming hot" Cheetos.

"I found the shapes were much more pronounced with the flaming hot ones," Huot reveals. "I don't know if they cook them differently or what, but something about those – the shapes are just much more interesting."

He's also not above using (and eating) the generic, store-bought brands – though he clarifies that they're not ideal for creating works of art. "The problem with off-brands is they don't have quality control," he clarifies. "They don't dust the coating as evenly. It's kind of distracting." Nonetheless, Huot admits they've yielded "some true gems." After all, it was in the depths of one of these bags that he "discovered" the Cheeto-bust of Mark Twain.

Regardless of the brand or flavor he uses, Huot says he finds "at least one shape in every bag" and sometimes as many as four or five.

When he finds a "showcase" piece, he photographs it, then stores it in an airtight tackle box for safekeeping. Though he acknowledges that his art form is impermanent, he testifies that the Cheetos have surprising staying power. "I have some that are eight months old and still perfectly fine," he says. "It seems like they actually gain strength over time – they take on moisture and get so stale that they're no longer brittle any more."

***

Recently, after being featured as an Instagram "suggested user" and amassing more than 40,000 followers, Huot decided to take his art to the next level.

In October of 2014, he set up an account with the online marketplace Etsy, through which he offers "very high-quality" prints of his creations for $20 to $25 each. It's a monetary amount that pales in comparison to the number of hours he invests in finding the shapes and photographing them. His first professional print, The Execution-Style Killing of a Man for Being Different, took him nearly two weeks to produce.

"It's a sad picture," he says. "It's enough to tear you up":

The Execution-Style Killing of a Man for Being Different

Huot's ultimate goal through Etsy is twofold: to spread the humor and beauty of his art and, more practically, to help fund his upcoming wedding.

"I haven't sold anything yet," he admits. "I'm new to Etsy, so I'm not sure how to master it. But also, I think people just don't know what it is."

"If they took a second to click on it," he adds, "they'd see that this is art."

Though Huot is a pragmatic engineer, he's always possessed the imagination of an artist.

"When I was in high school, my art teacher wanted me to go to some big art school," Huot recalls wistfully, "but I never pursued it because I always liked to build things too – and I thought engineering was more lucrative."

Cheetos reawakened Huot's creative soul and gave him an intense, cheese-coated purpose. To him, the lumpy cheese snacks are undoubtedly an art form:

*"I think art is something that you don't see
every day. You look at it and it makes you
feel something. It induces emotions.
Sometimes, it also makes you wonder
what the hell is going on."*

It's also a medium that comes with its fair share of doubts. "Sometimes I think, you know, 'What am I doing? Why am I wasting my time with this?'" he admits. "But when I read the comments, I realize it's all worth it."

"It's easy to think of this as a big joke," he adds, "but there's something magical in bringing Cheetos to life."

FOOD TRUCK ECONOMICS

Bobby Hossain's day starts early. Along with his family, he runs a food truck called Phat Thai that serves his mother's Thai recipes "with a modern twist." Although he won't serve customers for another four hours, he wakes up at 7:30am. He will work a double lunch and dinner shift in the truck, so his brother is on prep duty. Bobby buys any last minute supplies they need – ice, more bean sprouts – from Restaurant Depot while his brother cuts vegetables and slices meat in the kitchen space they use in a friend's restaurant. His brother then drives the truck to their parents' house. They load up and Bobby is on the road at 9:30am.

From 11 AM to 2 PM the brothers work at Mission Dispatch, a location in San Francisco's Mission district that hosts food trucks and draws a dependable lunch crowd. Bobby's mother cooks, his employee Frank takes orders, and Bobby hands out completed orders while helping the other two. After three hours, Phat Thai has served around 200 dishes.

Once the lunch crowd dies down, they return to the commissary, a space where they can clean dishes and dispose of garbage. Bobby checks whether he needs to buy more supplies, preps for dinner, and then drives the truck to North Beach in San Francisco. From 5 PM to 8 PM, they will sell Thai dishes at a "market" of food trucks organized by a company called Off The Grid. On busy days, Bobby won't have a chance to eat lunch.

Although it's only half as busy as lunch, Phat Thai

sells dinner to a dense crowd of families and professionals returning from work. By the time they serve their last customer, clean up, and park the truck, it's approaching midnight. It's one of Bobby's busiest days; he and his brother only do double shifts twice a week. On other days they don't serve dinner, and he can get home by five o'clock.

Bobby Hossain serves up customers during lunch rush

Food trucks like Phat Thai are a different breed than the original American food trucks (also known as roach coaches) that frequent construction sites and baseball stadiums. Instead of cheap, greasy fare, they sell $10 dishes featuring organic ingredients and fusions of different regional cuisines. Since they emerged as a media sensation in 2008, food trucks have asserted themselves as a force in the food scene, employing celebrated chefs and inspiring countless food reviews.

As a service that strips all the overhead costs of a

restaurant down to the minimum requirements for selling food to customers, food trucks also resemble lean startups: the Silicon Valley practice of quickly rolling out a minimum viable product, allowing customers to try it, and engaging with them to improve the product. Just as the falling cost of creating a website or app lowered the barriers to entry in the technology industry, food trucks allow aspiring restaurateurs to quickly put their creations in front of customers with minimal financial barriers.

Critics pan food trucks as a fad that tricks gullible hipsters into spending $10 on a sandwich served on a paper plate, while foodies defend them as a fun way to enjoy delicious and novel foods. But as long as customers keep coming, these mean, lean mini-restaurants will have a lot to offer aspiring chefs – and a place in the culinary world.

A Truck of One's Own

Countless restaurants exist around the globe, but running one is no simple matter. The omnipresence of restaurants means brutal competition for business; profit margins are notoriously thin. According to one well-cited study, 25% of new restaurants fail in their first year and 60% fail within their first three years. And while summing up the cost of a new restaurant is about as exact as giving a figure for a new house, one industry survey calculated the average cost of a new concept restaurant at $501,236 and the cost of taking over an existing restaurant at $281,128.

These factors are driving people in the restaurant business to explore food trucks as an alternative.

Bobby's family previously owned a Thai restaurant, but as Bobby bluntly explains, "The restaurant business sucks." With the possible exception of investor-backed restaurants with flashy concepts, it's nearly impossible to get traction. Bobby and his family paid $4,500 a month in rent, and with their daily customers numbering from 200 to as few as "a few," they hemorrhaged money too quickly to build up a customer base. Bobby explains:

> *"There's no rent control on restaurant rent, so even if we did start to be successful, the landlord could jack up our rent. A lot of restaurants get taken advantage of by landlords this way."*

After comparing the rent of the restaurant to the "rent" of attending food truck events like Off The Grid's markets ($50 plus 10% of sales), the decision to switch to a restaurant on wheels was an easy one.

The story behind Phat Thai is not unusual. The majority of San Francisco's food truck owners have a background in restaurants – the lone exception we met were several former DJs and promoters serving sliders – and by far the most common reason we heard from chefs for getting a truck was the desire to start their own business.

Although it is a major endeavor, it's much cheaper and quicker to start a food truck than a new restaurant. The process takes only several months, and at $50,000 to $150,000 in startup costs, the price tag is much more affordable than a restaurant's.

The biggest startup cost is the truck itself. Bobby's family bought their truck used for $37,000. Pelle, a caterer who sells Nordic dishes like meatballs, mashed potatoes, and lingonberries from his food truck, paid $20,000 for his used truck and another $27,000 to outfit it. Custom trucks, however, are a larger investment. To meet the challenge of cooking quality sushi, Thomas of We Sushi spent over $100,000. But while trucks are not cheap, given the healthy market for selling a used truck, buying one is not a terrible risk.

The other major expense is licensing and permits. Josh, the Communications Director of SOMA StrEAT Food Park, which hosts food trucks every day, estimates permitting costs in the Bay Area at up to $10,000, a figure confirmed by several truck owners. The various licenses include a business license, food handler certification, health certification, and fire certification. Many licenses are administered by the county or city, so a truck that wants to freely roam from the South Bay, north up to San Francisco, and east across the bridge to Oakland and Berkeley needs to clear the permitting and license requirements of at least four counties – an expense some but not all trucks undertake.

The owners we spoke to averaged two months of effort until they served their first customer. The maximum we heard was six months from a crew that was new to the restaurant business.

While starting a food truck is a commitment like any small business, it is quicker, cheaper, and less risky than a restaurant. For entrepreneurs like Bobby and his family, who paid $70,000 in startup costs, that means that financing the venture with personal savings is not out of the question. Josh, who knows dozens of truck owners from the StrEAT Food Park, stresses that the lower barriers to entry have enabled more minority, low-income, and immigrant chefs to start their own business. At its best, the food truck is a democratizing force of social mobility.

Necessity Meets Opportunity

The modern food truck has a founding narrative rooted in the Great Recession and the emergence of social media.

The popping of America's housing bubble in 2007-

2008 meant a stall in new construction projects, leaving food trucks without their best customers. Suddenly, hundreds of used food trucks were for sale. Simultaneously, the recession left many chefs unemployed and potential restaurateurs nervous about the risk of opening a restaurant.

Entrepreneurial chefs bought food trucks and began selling their creations on the street. Thanks to Facebook and Twitter, they could more easily reach customers and publicize their daily schedules and offerings. A creative cooking culture developed to lure foodies to food trucks. It became a media sensation, captured in social media as well as television series like the Food Network's "Great Food Truck Race." Where food trucks once housed only the lowest ranking kitchen workers, they began to feature talented chefs.

Supporting infrastructure also developed to fuel the growth of the food truck scene.

Food truck owners cannot run the business out of their house, as they are legally obligated to prep food and dump used "gray" water in a certified space. So commissaries began catering to food trucks, offering places to park and re-charge the trucks in addition to cooking facilities.

Organizations like Off The Grid and SOMA StrEAT Food Park offer trucks easy access to customers. Since the reputation and stability of the organizers draws a crowd, trucks can sell to many customers from day one. Some commissaries, like La Cocina, act as incubators for trucks and other food entrepreneurs, offering advice as well as space. We also spied "Mobi Munch," the name of a company offering a streamlined process of renting a ready-to-go truck, helping with menus and branding, and accessing profitable locations, on the side of several trucks. The pioneers of the food truck world, who established the norm of following trucks on Twitter and searching out their social media presence, also makes it easier for trucks to market themselves today.

By 2012, the food truck market brought in an estimated $1 billion in annual revenue. But regulation threatens the survival of the fragile food truck ecosystem.

In 2008, gourmet food trucks dealt with regulations designed for small numbers of trucks operating with low visibility. No cap on their numbers existed. They earned certifications and accessed popular spaces fairly easily.

As the trucks' presence increased in dense urban areas – and local governments faced the ire of restaurants decrying their loss of business to food trucks (which is unfair, in their eyes, as trucks keep costs low by selling on public land) and residents who sometimes dislike the presence of food trucks – regulations have become more onerous and some caps have been instituted. A food truck applying for a permit in Chicago today, Bobby notes, will receive one in eight years. Regulations in New York City have hindered the health of the food truck scene, and even The Economist has lambasted "how regulators keep cheap food out of hungry mouths."

San Francisco's regulatory response has been less severe. Yet regulation still leads to long waits for licenses; some trucks avoid the permitting process for street parking entirely and sell exclusively at private functions and marketplaces like Off The Grid. Between the increasing cost of buying a truck and the heightened costs of permits, Bobby says, the startup costs of a food truck in the Bay Area has doubled.

These changes have happened quickly. "A year is equal to 10 food truck years," Bobby tells us. Food trucks are uniting to fight the changes, and the efforts of companies like Off The Grid to secure space and permits for trucks is a great help. But just as Uber and

Lyft run afoul of regulation-protecting cab companies, restaurant-centric rules could curtail the delicious, grease-fueled growth of America's food trucks.

Street Food Culture

Food trucks are not only relatively cheaper and easier to start, they are also extremely lean.

Phat Thai has limited operating costs. It's mostly a family affair, with only one employee from outside the family. The main expenses outside of labor are $1,000 a week for food and supplies, $200 for insurance, and $120 to fill up the truck's enormous tank. Its engine is the same one that powered Camaros in the seventies, but even with its terrible gas mileage, a tank suffices for the week. Bobby's family borrows kitchen space in a friend's restaurant, but commissaries complete with a kitchen, waste disposal, and a parking space run up to $1,000 a month.

Another expense, for trucks that sell at places like Off The Grid, is the cut they owe to the organizers. Off The Grid charges ten percent – something of an industry standard. Off The Grid also expects vendors to sell a minimum of $1,000 of product over the course of a lunch or dinner period. So if a truck sells at Off The Grid for lunch and dinner, five days a week, the owner will pay the organizer a minimum of $1,000 per week.

It takes practice to purchase the right amount of food and not let any go to waste. Otherwise, there are few variables to a truck's costs. Success results from great food and solid branding and marketing. Customers can rest assured that they are not spending money on leather upholstery or a hostess who makes customers feel special. Food trucks rank as one of the most efficient ways to get food into people's mouths.

Yet while minimal costs are a major appeal for food truck owners, unlike with the roach coaches of the past, lower prices are not the main draw for customers. While several owners say their prices are around $3 cheaper than they would be in restaurants, food truck entrées still cost $8 to $12 and even desserts or snacks run $3 to $5. Instead, the scene that made food trucks trendy is based around experimental cuisine and the social aspect of street food.

In the high-risk world of restaurants, menus rarely change. But from the start in 2008, food trucks took advantage of the freedom of owning a truck to experiment. Rather than advertise a few dollar discount for tracking down a truck, they marketed the novelty of their creations and lured customers with the promise of fancy food at the price of a modest restaurant.

San Francisco's Off the Grid offers a wide array of 'noms'

Restaurants are still all about the mantra of "Location! Location! Location!" and tend to serve popular staples. Some food truck customers we spoke to, mainly those eating outside their office building, cited convenience as a factor for coming out. But especially at events like Off The Grid, where each truck is competing with three to twelve adjacent trucks, chefs compete on quality and creativity. Fusions of different cuisines are common, especially as low startup costs makes trucks affordable for immigrants. Most Indian restaurants feature Chicken Tikka Masala because it's a reliable crowd pleaser; Indian food trucks sell Chicken Tikka Masala burritos. Burger joints offer toppings like bacon or even a fried egg; food trucks sell peanut butter and jelly burgers with bacon and sriracha.

A collection of food trucks can also create a fairground atmosphere. Off The Grid cites an "asian night market," where street food brings neighbors and friends together in India, China, and Southeast Asia, as their inspiration. At their markets, they bring out chairs, play music, or put on live performances to make the market a community event. A number of the chefs we met cited the social aspect of running a truck – sharing their dishes, meeting different clientele every day, and seeing people actually follow their truck location to location – as their favorite part of owning a truck.

Customers we spoke to cited the variety, the quality of the food, and a desire to enjoy San Francisco culture as reasons they sought out food trucks. Exactly zero customers cited low prices as the reason they were eating from a food truck.

Room to Grow

Those who think food trucks are a fad expect peak food truck to soon set off a food truck extinction unlike anything seen since the demise of the dinosaurs. But food trucks seem to have staying power.

No one has good data on how many food trucks "make it." Staff at Off The Grid and the SOMA StrEAT Food Park perceive the failure rate of trucks as lower than in the restaurant business, as the industry's low costs allow even mediocre trucks to scrape by. Bobby, however, feels that trucks either succeed or fail. Of the three other trucks that started at the same time as his, two have failed.

But for Phat Thai, at least, a food truck proved a much more manageable business than a traditional restaurant. If we look at the expenses of Phat Thai in broad strokes, and imagine if the family members earned regular salaries, rented kitchen space instead of borrowing a friend's, and went to an Off The Grid market for lunch and dinner five days a week, the truck would need $6,577 in weekly sales. At $10 a dish, that translates to selling 132 meals per day. When we spoke to Bobby, he had sold over 200 meals during that lunch alone.

In addition, while restaurants pay full rent while trying to attract their first customers, food trucks at markets like Off The Grid get immediate access to customers at rates based on their sales. Once trucks do achieve name recognition, however, it opens up more lucrative possibilities. Many truck owners do around one third of their business catering private events – weddings included.

Starting a food truck business is not easy, but the consensus seems to be that there is room for growth. According to Josh, who worked at a food truck before joining SOMA StrEAT Food Park, which has rapidly grown its customer base over its first nine months:

> *"There is more demand from customers for food trucks than there is supply. The market is not saturated yet like with restaurants. Eventually it will be, but for now demand is huge."*

Portland, which may have the biggest food truck scene (at least proportional to its size) with over 20 hubs or "pods" where food trucks gather, may offer a glimpse of the natural limits of a food truck scene. Writers report trucks quickly popping up and disappearing. So while the food truck scene in places like San Francisco has room for new vendors, it will be harder to enter the business in the future when demand has been met.

In San Francisco at least, people in the business still feel part of a burgeoning scene. Dawn, who co-owns the Me So Hungry slider truck, left the music industry for food trucks to be part of something new. Josh describes the best part of his job as "Being part of this as it grows" and "Seeing food we haven't seen before."

The Future of Food Trucks

While food trucks are solid small businesses, they won't make anyone absurdly rich. As Pelle of the Nordic With A Twist food truck tells us, "To make good money, you need a liquor license." Restaurateurs may wax about their cooking, but they make their money at the bar. On average, drinks account for 30% or more of a restaurant's revenues at markups of 80% to over 100% for bottles of wine.

New York City has granted a food truck a liquor license, but only because the recipient's truck is actually an immobile vehicle. Alcohol is too carefully regulated by city and state governments for a truck to receive a license.

The conventional wisdom is that at $200,000 in yearly revenue, a food truck will break even. (When we spoke to Bobby, he estimated that at least half the trucks at Off The Grid that day had hit this revenue goal.) Around $500,000 in annual revenue equates to a good salary for a truck owner and "just making it into the [food truck] major leagues." The absolute maximum a very successful food truck can make in a year is around one million dollars.

Those figures are revenues, not profits, so even a single, wildly popular truck can never make someone a really high salary. For that reason, many truck owners view food trucks as a stepping stone to owning a restaurant and profiting from a liquor license.

But a second camp, in which Phat Thai plants its flag, sees food trucks as the more profitable venture. Bobby says his family makes good money from their truck – more even than they would in a restaurant. Bobby adds that he might like to open a permanent location "as advertising for the truck" or to compensate for the variability in a truck's sales. (Rain can cut sales in half, and trucks need to earn around 75% of their revenue during the peak season from April to October.) Similarly-minded owners describe their trucks as profitable and claim they are recouping their investment.

Curry Up Now has since expanded into three restaurant locations

To scale a food truck business, owners need more trucks or to expand into catering or a permanent restaurant. Rather than choose between a restaurant or food truck strategy, however, the current model seems to be to do both. Curry Up Now, which is something of a poster child for food truck success in the Bay Area, expanded from a food truck to a fleet of food trucks, a catering business, and two restaurants.

Regardless of whether chefs approach food trucks as a stepping stone to a regular restaurant or as a final destination, they bring something new to the food industry. For chefs, they represent an easier way to start a business; for customers, they offer creative dishes at modest prices; and for both chefs and customers, they enable a social and fun atmosphere that is built around an appreciation of food.

"You don't get rich owning a food truck," Josh from the StrEAT Food Park reminds us. "But no one enters the food business to get rich. You do it because you're passionate about the food."

THE SAGA OF YOGA JOES

"So, what's new with your life, man?"

The question, directed at Dan Abramson by his friend Paul, came over coffee on a muggy San Francisco day in October of 2013. And Dan had much to say.

Since the two had last met, Dan had gone through the wildest year of his life. With no knowledge of textiles or yoga, he'd launched his own company, Brogamats, and designed yoga mats that looked like "burritos, downward-facing logs, quivers of arrows, and other manly things." It had started as a personal mission for the large, hairy thirty-year-old: he'd wanted to make yoga more accessible to men. After months of pinpricks, fashion jargon, and printer issues, Brogamats had gone viral on Reddit, found their way onto the shelves of Urban Outfitters, and become a must-have item for hipster yogis.

After Dan told Paul this harrowing tale, the two started joking around. "Have you considered making any other yoga goods?" Paul asked. "Like, what about yoga action figures?" A humorous duel ensued, in which they discussed what poor creatures Dan could yoga-fy and immortalize in plastic – cats, dogs, superheroes, and the like.

And then, in a haze of lukewarm coffee and laughter, Dan had an epiphany: *army men*.

The little plastic men were perfect. Molded into crouching, throwing, and stanced positions, the toys already somewhat resembled various yoga poses; the platforms army men stood on could easily be reimagined as mats. Above all, recalls Dan, "they were way too serious and in need of some subversion."

He'd already launched a company – how hard could it be to make army men doing yoga?

Dissecting Joe

Dan Abramson's Yoga Joes blueprints

In the weeks following his revelation, Dan was so stoked that he could hardly sleep. First, he simply bought a bunch of army men to see if they were remotely close to exhibiting yoga poses. He spent long hours combing the Internet for army men sets, purchased giant bags for $20 a pop, and then, like a mad surgeon, retired to his basement to create a "Franken-Army." He sifted through the massive piles in search of similarities:

*"One army man who was throwing a
grenade kind of looked like he was doing a
'warrior II'; there was another guy with a
rifle who had a perfect 'warrior' leg – toe
pointed out and everything. There was a
general standing proudly with binoculars
who worked well for the 'tree pose.' You
know, things like that."*

To keep track of which men fit which poses, Dan
created an elaborate numbering system and drew out
diagrams to help with categorization. Then, he method-
ically matched the army men with their corresponding
yoga poses – each with a "little sticker on them, with a
number:"

Of course, the army men didn't fit any actual poses
exactly. Hell, they weren't even close. Dan's next step,
at the recommendation of a designer friend, was to buy
a heat gun and begin manipulating them by hand.
What ensued was perhaps the goriest battle ever fought
by plastic army men: limbs were dismembered, heads
were cut off, and torsos were burned, melted, and
twisted. No soldier was spared.

In Search of the Perfect Butt

For hours each day, Dan hunched over his workbench
in a creative, noxious haze. "The basement got really
plasticy," he recalls, uneasily. "When you melt this
stuff, the fumes are really toxic...my girlfriend was
freaking out about me inhaling it." Dan bought a
gasmask, flung the windows open, and returned to his
obsession – one that didn't initially garner much
respect:

*"I was looking for some work on the side
while running Brogamats, and had a job*

> *interview. The prospective employer
> asked, 'What do you do with yourself all
> day, Dan?' I answered honestly – 'Just
> hanging out in my basement, melting
> army men' – and I don't think he was too
> thrilled..."*

What's more, he soon encountered the immense difficulty of mimicking human gestures. "A shoulder would be completely wrong – it would be bulging out, completely off. It was incredibly hard."

But shoulders were the least of his worries: Dan couldn't, for the life of him, find a decent army man butt. While many companies produce army men sets, most come in stock poses (i.e. the guy with binoculars, the guy lying down with a rifle), which makes finding certain body parts particularly difficult – including the coveted ass. "None of them had a butt," Dan distressfully recounts. "I had ten or twelve sets of army men by that point, and was just scouring through them for any sign of a decent butt. My girlfriend thought I was crazy."

Then, Dan was graced with the first of many mini-miracles. Late one night, he stumbled across a special edition Iwo Jima army set online, "the one with the guys lifting the flag":

> *"I couldn't believe it – one of the guys had
> a butt, and it was sticking out. I bought
> about ten sets, just so I could use that one
> guy. I just cut the butt out, and made a
> downward dog and a child pose. It looked
> like crap, but I had it."*

Dissatisfied with his hacked up, superglued prototypes, Dan completely rethought his process. Days later, armed with technology, he tried again.

The 3D Revelation

Frustrated with his "Frankenmen," Dan switched up his strategy. Instead of attempting to physically manipulate the plastic men, he figured he'd do it digitally. He took a class on 3D scanning at TechShop (a community-based industrial equipment workspace), then ran his unaltered army men (the ones he'd numbered as being the closest to various yoga poses) through the machine. Still, the results were less than stellar:

> *"They always came out weird, bubbled, bulged. They looked really bad. Each one took 23 minutes to scan, and people kept walking by, making the machine shake, and screwing up the process."*

Then came Dan's second mini-miracle. While killing time waiting for a scan to finish, he perused YouTube and happened across a tutorial on Daz Studio, a 3D modeling program. In the 23 minutes it took his figurine to scan, he'd already learned the basics of the program.

Dan changed tactics once again: this time, he would build his army men from scratch, without scanning somebody else's. It proved to be a breakthrough moment.

In the program, he started with a 3D model of a "naked man" who could be manipulated easily with a cursor. After clicking and dragging the model into the yoga poses, Dan had to dress them in army attire. For this, he turned to a "seedy online community" that sells digital artifacts:

> *"It's a whole community of people selling objects and digital poses. A lot of them are*

really sexualized figures, and it's a pretty
weird world to get into – but I was able to
get through it."

The quest for World War II attire proved challenging – his first mock-up looked more like a "1700s colonial soldier" – and it took weeks to find the appropriate helmets, shirts, and cargo pants. Dan also wanted to strip his mini warriors of their weapons, so as to encourage peacefulness and focus.

Eventually, Dan enlisted a freelance industrial designer to help out with some of the 3D rendering. The temporary hire ended up coining the "Yoga Joes" brand name.

Next on his docket, Dan had to ensure that his army men were anatomically correct from a yoga standpoint. He reached out to his yoga instructor, Stephanie Stolorow, and sent off 3D photos from every angle of every pose for her to evaluate. "Some of the army men yoga poses looked a little exaggerated at first, but they were close," she tells us. "Kind of a Barbie effect – like an actual human body can't look in some ways that a plastic one can."

Once Stolorow gave him the go-ahead on the poses, Dan headed to Moddler, a 3D printing service in San Francisco's Dogpatch neighborhood. Here, he printed his first set of Yoga Joes in ten poses: downward dog, child's pose, meditation, cobra pose, headstand, warrior one, warrior two, crow pose, tree pose, and forward lunge (later discontinued). Each figurine ranged from $40 to $75 to produce, depending on software issues the printer encountered.

Dan was generally pleased with the results, save for one detail: a few of the figures, set on army men-like bases, didn't stand up straight. Digging deeper into his pockets, he commissioned another freelancer to design a 3D yoga mat for his little dudes to stand on.

Breaking the Mold

Armed with a great-looking set of yoga army men, Dan forayed into the final step of his vision: mass production. But at $40 to $75 each, 3D printing wasn't a viable option to accomplish his goal of making 2,000 of each figurine. He had to make a custom mold.

But in order to be approved by the mold company, Dan had to convert the 3D files from "a hollow shell to a solid piece of software" – a complex design issue that seemed impossible to solve:

> *"I scoured the dregs of Elance and oDesk to find someone who could do this one, specialized thing. I hired all these guys from India, Tunisia, Ukraine – nobody could do it. They said they could, then they'd just end up baffled by it."*

Finally, Dan found a guy in Boston (at a considerably higher hourly rate) who performed the task – all just to get a quote from Fathom, the molding company. The price came with sticker shock: since Dan was interested in a "family mold" (all of the army men in one mold), the first figurine would be $8,000, and each subsequent one would be $4,000. The mold for the yoga mat stands would be an extra $4,000, placing the grand total somewhere north of $40,000.

Kickstarting Yoga Joes

When big toy companies entertain an idea for a new product, they have the resources to conduct large-scale market research; Dan, as a lone ranger, turned to Kickstarter to test demand for his Yoga Joes. But to make his product stand out on the Internet, he needed a killer video.

The filming process was almost as complex as the creation of the toys. He connected with a comedy writer friend and a few former co-workers from his old ad agency. Together they wrote an ambitious script, which called for an array of oddities, including an "old white-bearded yogi," a mechanical bird, and a life-sized army suit. Then, Dan spent weeks working out the details – from the precise shade of his green face paint, to dealing with an "enterprising magician" who had a monopoly on the battery-powered pigeon market. (He ended up purchasing a wind-up rainbow-colored bird, painting it white, and reconstructing its delicate wings with parchment paper.) At times, he questioned his dedication:

> *"I was at a point where I was running out of money. I was doubting myself a little bit and started to think about what I was going to do for a living. But I also thought, 'This is an accomplishment: I'm making a green suit, I'm making a frickin' robot dove, I'm crafting a diorama of other action figures doing yoga, I'm hiring an old Indian man to pose on a beach.' All the things we wanted to do, we did."*

Between prototyping and videography, Dan had invested about $3,000 of his own money and hundreds of hours of his time – but for him, this was a small price to pay to carry out a childhood dream. "I've always wanted to make a toy," he told us. "Now I've made one."

But to see the vision through to the end, Dan needed $40,000 for his molds – a tall order for a freelance designer living in expensive San Francisco. He hoped the Kickstarter community could appreciate his idea.

With bright eyes, in the last days of September of 2014, Dan launched his Yoga Joes Kickstarter campaign. For a donation of $20, he offered a set of six army men, all in different poses: downward dog, child's pose, meditation, cobra pose, headstand, and warrior two. (Active duty and retired military personnel, who, Dan learned, often use yoga to cope with PTSD, were granted the set for half price.)

Like any enterprising Kickstarter creator, Dan voraciously emailed hundreds of news outlets and blogs in an attempt to get coverage. Aside from a few minor publications, nobody replied.

Nonetheless, Dan's campaign chugged along nicely at first. Friends and family poured in to support him, and by the end of week one, Yoga Joes had raised $10,000 – 25% of its goal. Things looked good. But after Dan exhausted his contact list, his campaign began to fall behind. Two weeks in, contributions stagnated at around $12,000. Dan began to lose hope.

Then, something miraculous happened: Kickstarter featured Yoga Joes as a "Staff Pick" and featured the product on its homepage. Dan's bright green, grinning face was now among the first things to greet visitors to the site.

Instantly, donations climbed – $15,000, $17,000, $20,000. Dan woke up to a pleasant surprise: Yoga

Joes was already halfway funded.

After Yoga Joes were featured by Kickstarter, which reaches some 13 million people every month, the media outlets that had initially rejected the toys began to declare them the greatest thing on earth. In rapid succession, *CBS News*, *Huffington Post*, *Fast Company*, and an assortment of Kickstarter review sites picked up Dan's campaign. An article on *This is Colossal*, a popular blog, was shared over 40,000 times on Facebook and Twitter.

With ten days still remaining on his campaign, Dan reached his goal of $40,000. And this was just the beginning of the madness.

Next, Yoga Joes was sucked into the vortex of viral content aggregators: *BuzzFeed*, *LaughingSquid*, *Boing Boing*, *Bored Panda* – all sites with massive social media presence and hundreds of thousands of readers. A week earlier, Dan had sat in despair; now, he incredulously watched the money pour in: $50,000, $60,000, $80,000, $100,000!

By the time the campaign came to a close, Dan had raised $108,065 from 2,879 supporters. But even with Yoga Joes amply funded, he couldn't yet celebrate: he had to fulfill the promise he made to his supporters – a delivery of some 16,000 figurines by Christmas.

From the conception of his toy to literally cradling his new-born resin prototypes, Dan had cared for his product for over a year. He'd toiled in toxic basements with heat guns, slogged through 3D modeling software, and risen at the crack of dawn to negotiate with overseas freelancers. Like his toy, he had straddled the divide between warrior and yogi: disciplined, focused, unrelenting. His journey wouldn't end here.

With his Yoga Joes samples safely tucked into his carry-on, Dan boarded a plane to China.

He had to go see a factory about making a toy.

LIFE AS A LEGO PROFESSIONAL

Sixty-five years ago, deep in the basement of a Billund, Denmark carpentry workshop, an impoverished toymaker named Ole Kirk Christiansen invented LEGO. More than 560 billion pieces later, the company has defined childhood for millions of kids across the globe. For some, though, the fun doesn't end post-puberty.

Adult Fans Of LEGO – or AFOL (pronounced "awful") – is a small but passionate confederacy of builders who refuse to believe LEGO is just for kids. One AFOL we spoke with says community members are "highly educated and/or intelligent, and have some sort of technical background." Many are engineers, computer programmers, and hackers who have no reservations over shelling out $2,000 on eBay for rare, limited-edition LEGO sets like an Ultimate Collector's Millennium Falcon. As Jamie Berard, LEGO's senior product designer, says, "Dad's gotta have his toy room too!"

For a select few in the AFOL community, playing with LEGO bricks has become more than a hobby: the best of the best have made a career out of it. Investigating three such jobs – model master builders, LEGO Certified Professionals, and industry "renegades" – reveals what it takes to be a pro.

LEGO Master Model Builders

The road to becoming a master model builder for LEGO is arduous, and the monetary payoff is limited.

It's also highly competitive: there are only 40 LEGO master builders in the world, seven of whom are American.

LEGO hand picks these builders and employs them at the company's Discovery centers and its seven LEGOLAND theme park locations. In most cases, the builders have to start from the bottom and work their way up; only the most skilled LEGO artisans achieve the honored title of master builder.

New hires start as apprentice builders – essentially "glue minions," according to a young peon who works at LEGOLAND Florida. They spend long hours adhering thousands of individual pieces together and work on maintaining the parks' various LEGO sculptures and exhibits. Promising apprentice builders are promoted to senior builders. They earn an additional $2 per hour, which bumps their pay from $10 an hour to $12 an hour, and assume additional duties: constructing models, overseeing daily procedures, and shadowing the master builders.

LEGO's website has the following job description listed for master model builders:

> *"This exciting role will have you designing, building, removing, installing, and repairing all models at the attraction. You will help teach others by running workshops, speaking with media, and participating in events. We are looking for someone with flair who has the ability to create a wide range of models. Must follow design briefs to build LEGO® models for displays and marketing promotions."*

LEGO typically looks for candidates with a bachelor's degree in either an art-related field (architecture, design) or engineering (mechanical, aeronautical, structural). Candidates are also expected to have some level of 3D modeling experience with programs like Maya, 3ds, AutoCad, and SolidWorks – tools that prepare a candidate for working on LEGO's custom-built, computer-aided design platform. Most importantly though, a candidate must have a strong portfolio that displays a variety of LEGO skills.

Building LEGO sculptures all day may seem cool, but these duties come with a few caveats. The $37,500 a year salary isn't stellar for a highly selective post that requires a tremendous amount of practice, energy, and time to secure. For those who wish to have true creative freedom, the master model builder position often proves to be constricting: the majority of projects fall within premeditated or corporate-affiliated themes like Superman, Spiderman, or Star Wars.

To boot, all LEGO-sanctioned creations must be kid-friendly – after all, that's the company's main constituency. Custom builders wishing to create more controversial or experimental works like, say, a zombie village, won't be amused for long.

***

Twenty-three-year-old Andrew Johnson, a DePaul University History major, was the youngest master model builder ever hired by LEGO.

He was selected to participate in the interview cycle, an "intense, three-round" process in which competitors are not told what they'll be constructing in advance. Andrew re-created a Picasso sculpture, built a small-scale model of Dr. Seuss's Lorax with a mere 20 bricks, and, in the final 45-minute phase, whipped together a violin and harmonica to secure his dream job.

Andrew says he prepared by improvising with LEGO bricks:

*"I don't buy the kits that come with in-
structions. I would just buy several of
those big tubs, dump them out and start
with a picture of something in my head. I
can't remember the last time I used instructions for anything."*

Paul Chrzan, a 40-year-old master builder from
Connecticut, offers the same perspective:

*"I tell people just build, build, build. Just
keep playing with the bricks. Don't build
the house and the spaceship. Build your
family pet. Build a family portrait. Go
beyond what people usually do with the
bricks. Because that's what we do."*

For those who seek more intensive preparation,
LEGO also offers an MBA program – Master Builder
Academy, that is – that provides the "skills, design
secrets, and advanced building techniques used by the
pros." Even so, graduating from the academy comes
with no guarantee of a job at LEGO.

LEGO Certified Professionals

An even more selective crew, LEGO Certified Professionals (LCPs), are full-time, freelance LEGO artists
who are "officially recognized by The LEGO Group as
trusted business partners." Currently, there are twelve
of them in the world.

LCPs are considered "international LEGO ambas-
sadors." While they are not official LEGO employees
and don't get paid by the company, they enjoy a
business to business relationship with LEGO.

The company endorses their skills and sells them
bricks in bulk; in return, the company gets to advertise

the incredible works of art these individuals produce. As freelancers, LCPs are hired by corporations, brands, and private individuals to make custom sculptures. A few are also highly respected artists who display their LEGO work in galleries across the world. They generally make better money than master model builders and have more freedom in their project selection. But as freelancers, this is contingent on their output.

The concept of independent, LEGO-approved builders was the brainchild of Sean Kenney. Once a disgruntled web designer for Lehman Brothers, Kenney left his job in 2003 to become a master builder. Two years in, he pitched the LCP concept to LEGO corporate, and they gave him a shot. Today, he's a successful freelancer, having been commissioned by the likes of Mazda and Google to create custom LEGO "installations."

Kenney says there's really no "standard process" for becoming an LCP, but he admits that the best approach is to first spend some time as a master builder at LEGOLAND – a route taken by nearly a quarter of all current LCPs. LEGO is extremely secretive about what it looks for in an LCP candidate, and it has released no information about how to become certified. One hobbyist surmises that "if you aren't already a well-known LEGO builder with years of experience," the company likely won't consider you.

***

Before he became a LEGO Certified Professional, Nathan Sawaya worked as a Wall Street lawyer and earned a salary in the mid-six figures. To de-stress after intense days, he returned to his apartment and fiddled around with LEGO bricks. In time, he got pretty damn good. He started a website, Brick Artist, where his friends could submit requests of things for him to LEGO-fy: portraits of children, movie characters, animals, famous works of art. Then, on a whim, he decided to "go to the big leagues."

In 2004, he entered a contest held by LEGO to find the best builder in the United States. To his surprise, he won. LEGO subsequently hired him as a master builder at the rate of $13 an hour – about what he made per minute as a corporate attorney. After a few years mastering his craft, he embarked on an independent career with the endorsement of LEGO.

Today, Sawaya has two studios – one in Los Angeles and one in New York. His work has been featured in Times Square's Discovery Museum, Time Warner Center, and a hodgepodge of other exhibits in 17 U.S. states. His workshop contains over 1.5 million bricks in every color, shape, and size imaginable, and he routinely has three or four concurrent builds going on.

Notably, Sawaya has built a ten-foot-tall replica of the Trump Tower in Dubai for Donald himself, and a four-foot bumblebee for pop star Ashlee Simpson. He'll charge anywhere from $2,000 to $100,000+ for his commissioned work, depending on the scope of the project. Sculptures may take him two days, or two months. Incredibly, Sawaya claims he makes more money as a LEGO artist than he did as a corporate lawyer; equally surprising, he also says his hours are longer.

Other LCPs see similar success. Dirk Denoyelle, a 47-year-old who was once a stand-up comic, says there is "real money to be earned in the LEGO business." He recently sold a LEGO village replica for $20,000.

Robin Sather, Canada's only LEGO Certified Professional, runs Brickville Design Works and oversees a steady stream of business and museum pieces: his works include a "giant Egyptian sphinx, dinosaurs, fantastic castles, and more." He attributes his success as a LEGO builder to his unorthodox development:

> *"If your peculiarities can survive your*
> *adolescent years, you're going to be okay.*
> *By the time I got out of college into early*
> *adulthood – yeah – I was [the] LEGO guy,*
> *and everyone knew it. I'm a businessman*
> *and a LEGO builder; my relationships*
> *with clients are mostly [business to*
> *business]."*

Sean Kenney, who *The New York Times* touts among the "artistic elite" of LEGO builders, specializes in "LEGO homeware." His most recent innovation, a series of LEGO-inspired lamps, has been widely praised by Good Morning America, NPR, and The Wall Street Journal.

The LEGO Black Market

Larry Pieniazek is a Technical Architect at IBM by day and a LEGO architect by night. He is neither a master builder nor a LEGO Certified Professional, but he operates Milton Train Works, a company that produces custom LEGO train kits, out of his basement. He's part of a small but faithful contingency of people who run unaffiliated, freelance LEGO businesses. Many of these folks have day jobs, but they consider LEGO building more than just a hobby.

Pieniazek has a wealth of knowledge; he knows everything there is to know about LEGO, its major players, its history and its secondary market "underbelly." While working as part of a team contracted by Kellogg to produce a lifesize Tony the Tiger, Pieniazek found himself in need of 100,000 bricks – many of which had to be bright orange. Without the wholesale brick access of an LCP, he had to seek out an alternative option.

He turned to a community of online "brick brokers," a group of about 3,000 sellers who buy sets and part them out, capitalizing on builders' independent needs. Pieniazek estimates that "about 10%" of these sellers make a full-time living this way.

He also says there is a customized market for just about anything LEGO: pieces, sets, printed designs, and paints. One custom set, Brickmania, even inspired a $53,000 Kickstarter fund to produce tank accessories, artillery, and customized "Minifigs" (the little LEGO men) who don camouflage and enviable mustaches.

Remaining unaffiliated offers greater flexibility to create sets that fall outside LEGO's preferred, kid-friendly territory. LEGO Certified Professionals, says Pieniazek, are not permitted to make custom sets:

> *"Part of their agreement with LEGO stipulates that they can't produce any competing sets that may be at odds with the company. As unaffiliated builders, we have a little more freedom to make the stuff LEGO wouldn't dare to, which is fun."*

On the fringe of the LEGO frontier are the "speculators" – those who anticipate the desirability of a new set, buy a few dozen, hoard them, and then sell them at a considerable profit when they go out of production.

These speculators, like other toy profiteers, sell their stock online or at conventions; good speculators are talented at predicting which sets will be hot years down the line. Pieniazek tells us that Star Wars sets always "appreciate nicely," and he should know: He recently flipped a "10030 Imperial Star Destroyer," originally a $300 set, for $999. His set could have sold for as much as $1,500, he says, had it not been water-damaged.

Pieniazek insists that his toy star destroyer profits aren't notable. "Cafe Corner," a highly desirable set produced in 2007, originally sold for $139.99. Today, a pristine, sealed set can fetch $1,500 – a nearly 10x (ten times the original price) profit. "There are dozens of sets, if not hundreds, that are good for 2x-3x," says Pieniazek. "Most any Star Wars set more than five years old is good for at least 2x."

Brickpicker.com is a LEGO investment site specifically crafted for brick brokers to navigate the market. The site offers pertinent financial advice – "LEGO Disney Princess Part 2: Will the Clock Strike Midnight on Your Investment?" – and provides an intricate ranking system that "utilizes licensed eBay Terapeak data to show the LEGO investor popular trends in the secondary market."

A variety of other sites like bricklink and brickset catalogue every existing LEGO set from the early 1960s to present and dole out standard market rates for collectors and sellers. Bricklink alone lists 279 million items that range from Indiana Jones mini figures to tiny door hinges.

LEGO as an Artistic Medium

For those who make a living with LEGO bricks, money isn't paramount: it's more about pushing the limits of creation and pursuing something they love. True fans recognize that LEGO transcends far beyond a mere toy, says Pieniazek, into the realm of art:

> *"LEGO is a medium: we have a palette –*
> *its shapes, arrangement of shapes, the*
> *colors they come in. It's as pure of an art*
> *form as can be. And like any art, the key to*

*good building is having a system in place,
knowing how elements interact. LEGO is
truly the best building system ever
invented; everything works together in so
many serendipitous, unintended ways."*

Upon viewing Nathan Sawaya's "Art of the Brick"
installation at Discovery Times Museum, *The New
York Times* art critic Edward Rothstein shares a similar
opinion:

*"In its pure form...the LEGO block is at
once the least technological toy around.
But in another way, it is also one of the
most technological, technological in the
original sense of the word, alluding to
craft and mastery — techne — the art of
making."*

In the end, Pieniazek supposes we're all makers
piecing together the bricks of life. Some take this more
literally than others.

CHEESEBOARD

"When the sixties finally ended in Berkeley, sometime around 1994, the only thing left standing from that bygone era was the Cheese Board."

– Alice Kahn, *The Cheese Board Collective Works*

Even on a Wednesday afternoon, the Cheese Board pizza shop does brisk business.

The line stretches around the block. But if you check the restaurant's reviews, or just get in line, you'll discover that this line moves very, very fast. A jazz trio noodling in the dining area entertains the waiting patrons. At the register, a smiling young Mexican man takes your order and then asks you to stand to the side. Seconds later, a woman with intricately-tattooed arms hands you your half-pie.

You sit down and realize she's given you a few extra slivers to munch on while waiting for your friend. You nibble one and decide you should have ordered a whole pie. ("I live in New York and already miss this pizza," one online reviewer wrote.) Maybe if your friend is late enough, you will. But who would have thought roasted sweet potato, pasilla pepper, lemon zest, and hard goat cheese would make such a winning topping combination? You were skeptical when you heard it was the only option today.

It shouldn't surprise you that the pizza is so good or that the line moves so fast or that the service is so friendly. The woman who handed you the pizza is one of the owners – she left a corporate job to run the place.

The young man at the register is an owner, too, and the pizza you're eating is his recipe. He's watching you out of the corner of his eye; if customers like the recipe enough, he and the other owners will discuss adding it to the regular menu. A third owner sits a few tables down. She made the dough for the crust this morning. Now she's here off-shift, grabbing lunch and checking out the band she booked.

The woman asking if she can bus your now-empty pizza tray is also an owner, as is the guy refilling the hot sauce and the man running pizzas back and forth between the oven and the counter. The young woman who will sweep up your crumbs when the store closes at 3pm, shortly before it opens again for equally brisk dinner hours at 4:30pm, is an owner in-training.

The Cheese Board currently has dozens of owners. And within the San Francisco Bay Area, over one hundred of the hippest, hardest-working foodies around own and operate another six affiliated bakery/pizzerias.

Not Your Average Hippie Entrepreneurs

Elizabeth and Sahag Avedisian could have been moguls if they wanted.

In 1967, the married couple opened the Cheese Board as a simple cheese shop on a "quiet corner of a small college town" that didn't yet serve pizza. At first it appeared ill-advised: the Avedisians didn't have any experience in retail, and they didn't know very much about cheese.

But this was Berkeley's bourgeoning "Gourmet Ghetto." There was a popular grocery co-operative a few blocks away from the shop in one direction. Two blocks in the other direction, the world's first Peet's Coffee & Tea – now a national chain and publicly-traded company – was just getting started. Most importantly, there was a growing market for the "authentic and imported" cheeses the Avedisians quickly learned about and stocked.

In 1971, Alice Waters opened Chez Panisse in the same neighborhood. Today, many consider Chez Panisse the best restaurant in the world, and Waters is a full-on celebrity. Not only has she written best-selling books, she's had best-selling books written about her. In 1992, she became the first woman named "Best Chef in America," and she has been hailed as the "mother of American cooking."

But in 1971, Waters was a fresh college grad who wanted to run a "little restaurant" and make a "good living." She has said that when she opened Chez Panisse, she "made sure the Cheese Board would be nearby, because I knew I would be among friends."

While Waters remained an artisan through her success, plenty of other hippie entrepreneurs grew companies like Peet's, Burt's Bees, and Ben & Jerry's into multi-million dollar corporations. But the Avedisians didn't want to run a multi-million dollar corporation. They didn't want to "run" anything, at least not by themselves or as executives.

Utopian ideas held sway in the 1960s and the 1970s, and many popular visions of utopia involved non-hierarchical power structures. In other words, people dreamed of a world without bosses. The grocery store up the street was a consumers' co-operative. Sahag Avedisian had lived on a kibbutz in Israel, and the Avedisians had mostly staffed the Cheese Board with their friends and patrons. As Alice Waters' statement implied, by 1971, the Cheese Board was more than just a cheese shop. It was a cornerstone of the community.

So, in 1971, the Avedisians sold their cheese shop to its six employees at cost. "It felt to me that Sahag and Elizabeth were just giving the place away," Tessa Morrone, a former member of the co-operative said. "I had never heard of anything like that."

Pat Darrow, the Cheese Board's first employee, recalled, "We were marching for peace, but we had not heard anyone say the owner should not make money off the workers. That was amazing to me!"

That same year, Waters opened her restaurant, and the Cheese Board helped inaugurate it. Waters described the moment in the foreword she wrote for The Cheese Board Collective Works cookbook:

> *"I know I will never forget the astonishing night when the merry collectivists, having stripped themselves naked, burst through the front door in the midst of dinner service and streaked through the restaurant, the very embodiment of ecstatic, anarchic nature, if not anarcho-syndicalism."*

By then, the Cheese Boarders were "collectivists," and the Cheese Board was a "collective." The pay structure was completely egalitarian: Everybody earned the same wage, no matter how senior they were. They made decisions about the shop's operations through some form of consensus, even if it made for some very long meetings. This operating model and pay structure remain the same today.

Cheese Shop + Bread + Toppings = Pizza

Through its early years, the Cheese Board sold only cheese. Authentic, imported cheese.

Then, in the mid-1970s, a few members of the collective started making bread to occasionally serve with cheese samples. Baking bread requires a completely separate skill set from buying and selling cheese, so for a while the quality of the loaves hovered between "interesting" and "terrible." But flour is cheap, and as the bread was free, customers couldn't complain. And the bakers didn't have to worry about the management yelling at them, because they were the management.

They kept baking, and they got better. Eventually they made loaves good enough to sell, and just like that, the Cheese Board was a bakery. A popular bakery. An early Cheese Board member recalls, "Back when we first started making baguettes, almost nobody [in Berkeley] knew what a baguette was. Ten years later, you would see as many people walking around with a baguette under their arm as you would in Paris."

Once you have cheese and bread dough in the same kitchen, it's only a matter of time before somebody makes pizza. It happened in 1985, when business was slow and pocket change was scarce. As The Cheese Board Collective Works tells it, the first Cheese Board pizzas were made as an economical staff lunch:

> *"Someone grabbed cheese from the case, someone else would run next door to the Produce Center for vegetables. A half hour later, pizza was served. Customers noticed and wanted a piece, too. Before we knew it, we were selling slices for lunch."*

Today's recipes echo these beginnings: fresh vegetable toppings and high-quality, exotic cheeses on a sourdough crust. Sauce is usually only included as a garnish, to taste. The bakery only offers one combination of toppings each day, though the pizza-of-the-day varies widely within a given week.

Pizza sales pulled the Cheese Board out of a recession-era slump and turned business around in a big way. Pizza was such a financial boon that the Cheese Board opened a dedicated pizzeria in 1990. This pizzeria now has a space of its own, adjacent to the cheese shop and bakery. The members opted to take a temporary pay cut so they could have the funds to acquire and remodel the space when it became available. Even though the line for pizza moves very fast, it often curls round the block.

Business is booming, but as explained in The Collective Works, the Cheese Board owners aren't interested in expanding further:

> *"We want to promote worker coopera-*
> *tives, but not at the risk of changing our*
> *own scale or culture. Some of our lack of*
> *ambition can be attributed to a philosophi-*
> *cal distaste for society's dependence on*
> *and glorification of growth and expansion,*
> *and some can be because of our natural in-*
> *clination to take it easy, and keep things*
> *on a smaller scale."*

Still, it's hard to keep something so successful from spreading – in one way or another.

A Cooperative of Cooperatives

In 1995, one of the Cheese Board's owners wanted to open his own bakery pizzeria that followed the same, co-operative model. Along with a lawyer and a professor, he approached the Cheese Board asking for a loan and the advisory support to start a new bakery and pizzeria. The Cheese Board owners agreed.

"It's not really in a cooperative's interest to expand," says Maddy Van Engle, who helps run a network of cooperative bakeries that now includes the Cheese Board and this bakery.

There are no high-pay, top-level executives at the Cheese Board, pushing for major expansion. Everybody is both a top-level executive and a bottom-level laborer. A coop may aim to maximize profits, but its main motive is for its owners to sustainably earn a good living, on their terms. Sometimes, expansion is a threat to that goal. Consensus meetings of the 50 current Cheese Board owners are already a challenge – 50 more would likely require restructuring the organization.

But even though the Cheese Board owners didn't want to grow larger, they did want more worker co-ops to exist. "This was a way for them to help create new jobs and spread their business model," Van Engle explains, "without making their own operation too large to function."

They established the new bakery pizzeria (opting to stay out of the cheese retail business) in the adjacent city of Oakland in 1997. They named it "Arizmendi," after Jose Maria Arizmendiarrieta Madariaga, a Spanish priest who founded the Mondragon network of cooperatives, which today have a collective workforce of over 100,000 and comprise the seventh-largest corporation in Spain.

Arizmendi, the Oakland pizza bakery, was a success, and the owners paid back their loan to the Cheese Board. In 2000, a mere three years after the first loan, the two bakeries decided to do it again, and opened a second Arizmendi in nearby San Francisco.

Today, the Arizmendi Association of Cooperatives is made up of six cooperative bakery pizzerias distributed across the San Francisco Bay Area. Taking their inspiration from the Mondragon Corporation, the

Arizmendi Association is essentially a cooperative of cooperatives. One function of the Association is to help develop new cooperatives – historically, more bakery pizzerias on the Cheese Board model. Member cooperatives also pool their resources to support one another.

"The bakeries are all separately owned and run, so they all run differently," Van Engle explains. "Some of the older ones have a little bit less structure, the newer ones have the most structure – as the bakeries have been created, more and more lessons have been learned." Each cooperative has its own staff (who own the bakery they work at), its own menus (some sell more than one kind of pizza, for example), and its own wages (mostly a function of how well the individual bakery is doing). Not every bakery discloses wage information, but at the time of writing, owners of the Arizmendi in San Francisco's Mission district make around $20 an hour in wages (there's also a tip jar).

When it comes to decisions like whether to start a new bakery or change policies that affect more than one member bakery, they are made by the Association's "Development and Support Cooperative" board. Besides Van Engle and two more full-time members, the board of the Association consists of two bakers from each bakery (12 bakers total). The member bakeries pay dues to the Association to support "new jobs in the future, and to fund legal, financial and personnel support, whenever it's needed."

Van Engle was once a baker, too. She started working for Arizmendi bakery in 2010 as a baker without any baking experience. "Before that, I taught cooking and gardening to kids," Van Engle says. "All of the work that I've done had to do with food justice." She became deeply involved in the organizational aspects of the bakery, so much so that she was elected by the board to work for the Association full-time.

Though she's only been in the network four short

years, Van Engle says she's learned a lot – and not just about pizza. "Not having a boss is challenging, in a really interesting way," she says. "Most jobs involve trying to appease your boss, and bosses are supposed to manage workers below them to prevent conflict. But in a co-op, in a way, you have 20 bosses telling you 20 different ways to do things. And all the conflict comes up to the surface." When it does, members have to learn how to deal, or else the bakery can't function.

Van Engle says conflicts like these are more easily solved when everyone has a common cause they care about – in a cooperative's case, that cause is the continued success of the coop. It also helps that virtually everyone has a deep understanding of the business. "Everyone's doing everything," she says, referring to the fact that each baker/owner is trained for, and often rotates into, many different aspects of running the company. "Everyone's washing dishes, everyone's management, everyone's front and back of the house.

People feel a lot of ownership," she says. "People really care."

PRICEONOMICS

WHY THE LUCKY STIFF

"When you don't create things, you become defined by your tastes rather than ability. Your tastes only narrow and exclude people. So create."

– Why the Lucky Stiff

From 2004 to 2009, one of the most prolific programmers on the Internet went simply by the moniker "Why the Lucky Stiff" or by his Twitter username "_why."

Few knew who "_why" was in the real world, but his online persona was a force to be reckoned with. He built and authored dozens of free tools to help people learn to program, mostly in the Ruby programming language, which spread like wildfire, partly due to his influence. And he did it with a sense of humor. His text book, which he posted for free online, was titled *Why's (Poignant) Guide to Ruby*. "Poignant" because he wanted to teach people to write code so beautiful it made them cry. To this end, the (Poignant) Guide's narrator claims that the book, which most people read as an e-book, "comes with an onion":

> *"So you're like, 'Wow, this book comes with an onion!' (Even if you don't particularly like onions, I'm sure you can appreciate the logistics of shipping any sort of*

produce discreetly inside of an alleged
programming manual.) [...]

I'll be straight with you. I want you to cry.
To weep. To whimper sweetly. This book is
a poignant guide to Ruby. That means
code so beautiful that tears are shed. [...]
You really must sob once. Or at least snif-
fle. And if not, then the onion will make it
all happen for you."

He also made Try Ruby, a free, interactive website
that walked a beginning programmer through the very
first steps of learning, as well as a programming environment for children to learn to code that he whimsi-
cally named Hackety Hack. His publications had funny
illustrations in them of animals and rock stars. The
(Poignant) Guide even came with an original indie-rock
soundtrack, which included songs about bacon.

Cartoons from "Why's (Poignant) Guide to Ruby"

As Steve Klabnik, one of _why's collaborators, has
been quoted as saying: _why was not a "programmer,"

he was "an artist whose medium was code."

An air of mystery surrounded Why the Lucky Stiff, who became the closest thing the programming world had to Batman. His audience appreciated him enough that they respected his choice to conceal his offline identity. When invited to speak at conferences, he would register under a pseudonym, pay in cash, and jokingly wear sunglasses to half-heartedly conceal his appearance.

Then, one day, Why the Lucky Stiff completely disappeared.

***

Just before his disappearance, _why's anonymity was compromised. An anonymous blogger had combed the early records of _why's online communities, his patent records, and his associated IP addresses. The blogger presented, in incredible detail, proof that he had discovered _why's real identity.

As it turned out, _why was some guy in Utah who worked for a consulting firm. On the Internet, he was a legend. In the real world, he was no Bruce Wayne – just another normal person.

With his name revealed, _why did something that shocked the programming community: he committed digital suicide. He scrubbed himself from the Internet. His open-source repository and all its code, his blog, his applications, his books, and his Twitter account – he deleted them all. It appeared that Why the Lucky Stiff, the beloved performance artist of the programming world, had given his last performance: a vanishing act.

This devastated the multitude of programmers who relied on his work. Some people were angry to be left in the lurch, but more just felt sad that his art was gone.

These fans immediately launched an effort to

salvage the deleted material from the digital detritus. _why hadn't made any effort to hand off his projects, which meant nobody was responsible for keeping his important projects like Hackety Hack and Try Ruby up-to-date. Why the Lucky Stiff also wasn't great at leaving comments in his code, so inheriting one of his projects meant going through it, line by line, and figuring out what each function was for.

Over the past five years, many of _why's projects have flourished in the hands of others. And many of these successors have noted that their success depended on their eventual willingness to delete the code _why authored. As Steve Klabnik, who inherited Hackety Hack, told a Slate reporter, "_why's programming just really is not very good."

"That doesn't mean he wasn't brilliant," he added.

***

When most programmers call code beautiful, they mean that it executes its task efficiently and that it's easy for other programmers to read, work with, and build upon. By this standard of beauty, much of _why's code is very ugly. But _why's brilliance was that despite being so wildly creative that some people questioned his sanity, he channelled that creativity into code that people actually used.

As Diogo Terror wrote in his article, "_Why: A Tale of a Post-Modern Genius," it's much better to articulate your ideas than to worry about articulating them perfectly: "He just creates things and gets them out there in the wild, unafraid whether people think it's 'crappy' or 'unprofessional.'"

In short, _why took risks. He once expressed, "If you worry too much about being clean and tidy, you can't push the boundaries (I don't think!)" So he published imperfect things, and many people found many of them useful. While some of his products weren't particularly well-built, they were useful enough that others later spent time rebuilding them. Adults and children still learn how to program using his tools, he's still quoted and revered, and his books still teach and entertain.

Most people who become as famous as _why try at some point to turn their fame into money. Instead, _why chose to remain anonymous. When that was no longer an option, he dissolved his Internet persona completely.

***

_why's most recent project, or at least, the project most recently attributed to him, is a brief novel. It was published when his old blog, whytheluckystiff.net, came back online for a few months displaying only one, cryptic line of code: "Public Print Queue SPOOL/DES-OLEE 2012-01-06T08:21Z." Then, for one day in April, the website listed a series of printer commands which, if executed, printed out the 84-page document. The site went offline a day later, and the url now hosts a seemingly unrelated Australian's personal blog.

In the text, the author of the novel claims to be _why – a claim that many people accept. The author discusses his disappearance, pseudo-anonymity, and his relationship to programming as an art form. He expresses remorse. He says his intent in writing the novel is to open-source the character of _why as he once open-sourced his code – putting _why's manifesto into the world, as flawed as it might be:

> "I want to make it perfectly clear that
> these papers and all my other works in life
> belong to the general public. In fact, I also
> would like to turn myself over to all of you

as well. This was actually done several years ago, but in an embarrassingly disorganized manner. I like what you've done with the character, but I'd like to step into his tattered suit for the next hundred pages and a day. And after that, I'm yours again. Do what you must do! I always enjoy seeing what happens to me."

STARTING A BIKE SHOP

The story of Huckleberry Bicycles begins with a corporate lawyer named Brian Smith. Like most corporate lawyers, Brian was miserable, and he wanted to start his own company. He teamed up with Jonas Jackel, a friend of his since college and an experienced bike shop guy. Jonas then recruited another bike professional, his friend Zach Stender. Together, they planned to start San Francisco's newest bike shop.

But San Francisco doesn't exactly suffer from a shortage of bike shops, so it wasn't clear that the idea for Huckleberry Bicycles was a slam dunk. The three founders had also decided to open their shop in San Francisco's Mid-Market District, one of the highest crime areas in the city, which retailers traditionally shun. This meant the three friends faced all the traditional challenges of starting a business, and an additional unknown: Amidst the drug dealing and strip clubs, could they sell speedy commuter bikes and stylish cycling pants?

Financing the Shop

On day zero, when Huckleberry Bicycles only existed in the founders' imaginations, Brian, Jonas, and Zach calculated that they would need $300,000 to $350,000 to get started if they managed their costs aggressively and did a lot of the work themselves. The seed money would allow them to find and renovate a retail spot, buy initial inventory, hire a first employee, and provide a buffer to last at least a year.

As two of the founders were former bike shop employees, they had a fairly accurate idea of what costs to expect. They projected that they would need a 2,000 square foot store, which in a less expensive neighborhood, would cost $6,000 to $8,000 in rent each month. Renovating the store would cost roughly $100,000 – they would do most of the work themselves. They budgeted $75,000 for initial inventory and $25,000 to $50,000 for miscellaneous expenses. That left $100,000 as a buffer, so they could confidently hire a full-time employee to run their service center.

The founders put in a small amount of initial capital, but they needed to raise most of the money. They considered bringing in additional investors, but they ultimately decided that it didn't make sense to give away more of the company when they needed relatively little financing.

The year was 2010, which was a tricky time for a new small business to raise money from banks, as they had tightened lending requirements after the 2008 financial crisis. The founders were willing to personally guarantee the loan and had good credit and personal assets. The company, on the other hand, had no financial history or assets for a bank to review.

In an unexpected twist, the San Francisco city government helped get Huckleberry Bicycles on the road. When members of San Francisco's Office of Economic and Workforce Development heard that several gentlemen wanted to start a bike shop on a decrepit stretch of Market Street, they connected the friends with a lender willing to underwrite the loan and introduced them to their eventual landlord.

***

Launching Huckleberry Bicycles

With the financing and a location in place, Brian, Jonas, and Zach started converting a dilapidated storefront located next to a strip club into a haven for urban cyclists.

First, they needed bikes to sell. The bike industry operates a lot like the car industry. Bike manufacturers like Cannondale and Trek sign contracts with bike dealers to give dealers exclusive rights to selling the bikes in geographic areas. This insulates the dealers from competition and allows the manufacturers to set prices. Almost no companies allow their brand name bikes to be sold online.

The first bike manufacturer that Huckleberry talked to backed out just before signing the contract; the manufacturer worried that another one of their existing dealers was located too close to Huckleberry Bicycles. Luckily the friends signed up other bike vendors fairly easily. As it turns out, companies like to work with people who want to sell their products! In quick succession, the founders signed up vendors like Cannondale, Felt, Masi, and Public Bikes.

Most bike manufacturers offer dealers a line of credit to finance their inventory with a 0% interest rate as long the dealers pay for their bikes in time. (The period of the loan can vary from 30 days to six months.) Still, dealers purchase about half the bikes in their inventory immediately and buy all "soft goods" like biking clothes, locks, racks and lights outright, so dealers need a decent amount of upfront cash to stock their stores.

Prices and margins are fairly standardized across the industry and can't really be controlled by bike stores. The average retail gross margin on bike sales is 36%, which means a store that sells a bike for $1,000 will make a profit of $360. For soft goods, the industry standard margins are 50%. The average bike store earns 40-42% margins since they sell a mix of bikes and soft goods.

Since the margins are predictable, the founders' revenue projections gave them a good idea of how much profit margin they could devote to paying salaries and rent. The business would need to hit certain sales goals or it would predictably implode.

One year after Brian quit his job at a law firm, Huckleberry Bicycles opened for business.

A Year in the Bike Business

Like many new business owners, the founders had to be told by a seasoned professional that their expectations for the bike shop were too optimistic. As Brian explains:

> *"Before we got started, we made all these aggressive predictions about our revenue. We met with an accountant, and she was like, 'Get out of here, these numbers are crazy.' So we went back and made much more conservative assumptions."*

Unlike most new business owners, however, the three founders' optimism was not misplaced. The first year went really well, and Huckleberry's sales exceeded even their more aggressive set of projections. Still, Brian maintains that listening to their accountant was a good idea. "It was good to be conservative," he says. "Otherwise we might have made bad spending decisions."

Three months in, the founders could start paying themselves. Eight months later, they could afford to pay themselves a livable wage. Better yet, they could enjoy the thrill of seeing their hard work pay off:

"Yeah, I remember the first bike we sold, it was awesome. I remember our first $1,000 day and that felt incredible. Then we had a bunch of really big sales days and you need something even bigger to get the same rush."

Soon a team of four couldn't handle all the business walking in the door. The friends kept hiring another hand until the team grew to twelve people. Every time they added a new team member, the investment paid for itself with extra sales. The founders haven't touched the $100,000 buffer that they budgeted when they started the company. Moreover, their initial budget of $300,000 to $350,000 to launch the business ended up being extremely accurate.

Despite all their success attracting business, the Huckleberry team can't pinpoint how they acquire customers. "Every time someone walks in the door, we give them the best possible experience, and we really do make them happy," says Brian. "But why do more new people walk in each day? I don't really know."

The three founders have bought Google and Facebook ads, but they have no way to track how they convert. The store is located on a main bike thoroughfare, so commuting bikers can discover the store. But it's also in a bad neighborhood, so it's hard to know whether the location helps or hurts. The team tries to really satisfying every customer so people will learn about the bike shop by word-of-mouth, but it's impossible to measure how much providing great customer service impacts sales.

In many ways, starting Huckleberry Bicycles was a leap of faith: if you build it, they will come. And they did. All the investments the friends made in more staff and more inventory have paid off. They just can't say why exactly.

The Bike Shop's High-Tech Toolkit

Although the technology in bike stores usually has to do with lighter bike frames rather than software, the Huckleberry team runs its entire business on cloud-based business applications they can use from any web browser. This includes Google Apps for Email, Quick-Book Online for bookkeeping, and Square for payment processing.

The most important piece of software in their business is a point of sale and inventory management system called MerchantOS. They rave about it. It only costs $50 a month, and it has a solution specifically for bike shops. The app tracks the store's inventory and also tracks the inventory that its vendors carry. So, for example, if a customer asks for a specific bike rack, the Huckleberry staff can instantly check if it's in stock in the store or if they can order it from one of their vendors to make the sale.

The founders also spent $10,000 getting a website up. (They originally paid $6,000 for the site, but they didn't love the result, so they had it redone a few month later.) They sell some accessories online on a Shopify online store, but it's not an emphasis. And while they mention the bike brands they carry on their blog so that people sometimes show up at the store because they Googled "cannondale san francisco," they don't bother showing their entire bike inventory online.

Huckleberry isn't trying to be the world's best bike website, so the maintenance and mental overhead of keeping inventory online isn't worthwhile. Software tools have really helped the Huckleberry team. But the shop will succeed or fail based on the customers' experience in the shop, so that's what they want to nail.

***

Contemplating Success

It's commonly asserted – and presumably true – that most retail businesses fail. The competition is intense, labor costs (especially in San Francisco) are high, and customer demand can be fleeting. The founders of Huckleberry Bicycles took a large risk in starting a bike shop, which Brian describes as a factor that pushed them to work so hard:

> *"If I had started this business projecting that we'd fail, we wouldn't have started it. It's not an option to fail. My partners have kids and houses. It's not an option."*

Today, that hard work has paid off. Entering Huckleberry Bicycles, it's immediately clear that the staff puts extra effort into helping novice bikers and insane randonneurs alike. Customers can even play Tetris when they need a break from checking out bike frames and imagining how their derriere will look in that pair of racing shorts.

Even in the biking mecca of San Francisco, the store manages to feel unlike any other bike shop. And for the founders of Huckleberry Bicycles, a bike shop cheerfully growing and selling a bright array of bicycles in a neighborhood that many residents disparage, that was the plan all along.

HOW TO GIVE HALF YOUR
WORK AWAY FOR FREE

When Matthew Manos was 16-years-old, he decided he wanted to be a designer.

So, he did what any aspiring teen entrepreneur would do: he bought a Mac. Then, he enrolled in a digital art class and spent long nights learning Photoshop, Illustrator, and InDesign. He began with the usual stuff – like rendering his friends' faces onto cats – but soon craved more fulfilling work. A few months later, while hanging out at his local skatepark in Sunnyvale, California, an opportunity arose.

"Down in the bowl, this guy was doing flips in his wheelchair," Manos recalls. "I was super interested – I had to meet him."

As Manos approached, he realized the man wasn't alone: a small group of children in wheelchairs followed him through the park, grinding down pipes, flying down slopes, and swiveling with reckless abandon. The man, it turns out, was running a non-profit – then known as Wheelchair Skater – that encouraged disabled children to participate in extreme sports. After speaking with him, Manos offered to make promotional stickers for the non-profit.

It was his first design project, and he did it for free.

"To be honest," says Manos, "I never imagined how pivotal a moment the creation of those silly stickers would have on my life at the time."

Today – a decade later – Manos is the founder and

managing partner at *verynice*, a design firm that gives 50% of its work away for free to nonprofits like Unicef, Human Rights Campaign, and the Keep A Breast Foundation. He's built a team of 350 volunteers and contractors that has saved not-for-profit organizations in 45 countries over $1.5 million in design services.

And perhaps most importantly, he's mapped out his entire business model so that others may follow suit.

Uninspired Beginnings

While pursuing his undergraduate degree in design from UCLA, Manos says he was indoctrinated with industry stereotypes: designers don't start businesses – they brand businesses; they don't create products – they package ideas; they don't build communities – they design housing.

He was told that this system was inherently static: it was a business's role to make money, and businesses employed the designer solely to help sell its products. For years, Manos had known that he wanted to start a business, but as he was exposed to the "reality" of the design landscape, he grew skeptical.

For some time, he steeped himself in the theory of social design, which posits that a designer has a "responsibility to bring about social change." But as he researched, he found that while most "social" design firms claimed to work toward benevolent causes, they still charged non-profits substantially for contracted work:

> *"I learned that nonprofits in the U.S. alone spend $7.6 billion on marketing and design every year," he recalls. "And I thought: why not provide nonprofits with free design work so they can directly reinvest that money toward their causes?"*

"A nonprofit's mission is not to have beautiful website – it's to save the world, to do noteworthy things," he adds. "It shouldn't be spending money on things not tied to its mission."

With many questions, he set out to address these issues.

Step One: Work Really Damn Hard

In 2009, during his last year of college, Manos set out to offer his design services at 100% pro-bono rates to nonprofits. He launched his own company, *verynice*, and "naively" scrawled his early working company motto on a dinner napkin: "Save the World." (This would later morph into "Change the design industry through disruptive innovation and authentic intention").

He spent his nights, weekends, and virtually all of his free time providing work for his clients at no cost – simply for the joy of making a positive difference. He had no employees, managed all of the work himself, and thoroughly enjoyed himself while doing it – though the initial jobs were "small and irregular."

A year later, the summer after he graduated from UCLA, Manos had his first "big break": he won a bid to design the promotional materials for MTV's horror film, Savage County. The big-name boosted his credibility substantially, and work for both nonprofits (pro-bono) and small businesses (paid) trickled in.

When Manos began his MFA program that fall, he faced the precarious challenge of balancing coursework and running his business full-time. "It was absolutely horrible," he laughs. "I'd get to school at 4 AM, work on my company until 10 AM, then do school stuff the rest of day until 5 or 6 PM."

All the while, he began to develop a more focused business model.

Though Manos enjoyed his nonprofit work, a 100% pro-bono design company would not work. But he also didn't want to create a company that mostly did paid work for corporations just like everyone else. Ultimately, he settled on a middle ground: he'd run *verynice* as a for-profit corporation that donated 50% of its work for free to nonprofits.

***

The concept of giving away free stuff is nothing new, admits Manos. In the 1880s, Coca-Cola offered the first coupon, which promised a free glass of soda. Within 10 years, one in nine Americans had consumed the beverage, largely thanks to the company's promotional giveaways. Consumers in the 1950s were inundated with "buy one, get one free campaigns" from nearly every competing brand. In the last few decades, businesses like Tom's Shoes have given this model a philanthropic twist by donating one product to a child in need for each product purchased.

These concepts, however, were rarely applied to the service industry, where the cost is not simply rooted in manufacturing, but involves employees' time. When Manos first proposed his idea of giving away 50% of his design work, others scoffed at it. "A lot of influential people told me it was a bad idea," he says. "They'd tell me, 'Don't give work away for free – it devalues your design, and it's hurting the economy by taking jobs away!'"

For Manos, it was a "moral, ethical decision" – something he felt was his duty as a designer. But a glaring question remained: how could he afford to give away his work for free?

***

A *verynice* Business Model

After much thought, Manos had an answer: "if you want to give half your work away for free and do just as well as the next guy, the simple equation is that you have to do twice the amount of work that they do."

In other words, he'd do twice as much paid work in order to devote 50% of his work to nonprofits at no cost. Manos calls this the "double-half" methodology:

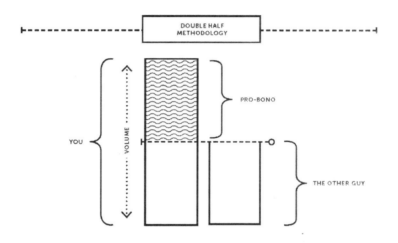

In order to make this model work, Manos needed to build out "an innovative approach to capacity building." He knew he'd have to get creative with out-sourcing work and that he'd have to build a large network of remote contractors and volunteers keen on providing their services for free to nonprofits.

The process proved to be surprisingly organic. "As soon as we launched our website, we got our first volunteer, a designer based in D.C.," Manos says. "What made it special is that she just approached us without us even posting a listing." Ironically, adds Manos, this differed greatly from the "volunteer canvassing" and guilt-tripping utilized by most of the nonprofits he hoped to help.

As Manos signed on notable nonprofits like Amnesty International and the Human Rights Campaign, his pool of volunteer applicants, hungry for exposure and experience, grew tremendously. By the end of 2012, he had a remote *team* of 100 contributors – almost all of whom did both pro-bono work for nonprofits and paid work for for-profit companies with *verynice*.

"Our volunteers make a social difference, and have the opportunity to gain valuable experience" says Manos. "What's more, when you do something for free, you have more creative control over your vision – it allows for the piloting of experimental ideas."

The influx in nonprofit work also made *verynice* visible to for-profit companies willing to pay for great design work, says Manos:

> *"We were working with a nonprofit in Orange County (CA) for long time...and in the course of things, we spent a lot of time with their Board of Directors – one of whom was involved at Disney. He got to see what we were capable of through the whole process, and when a project popped up at Disney, we were the first company he thought of, and we were hired for the job."*

Disney wasn't a unique case: the boards of most large nonprofits teem with CEOs of massive for-profit corporations, so *verynice* can often segue into paid work though these connections. Nonprofits also tend to have hundreds of volunteers with day jobs, adds Manos, and they often set *verynice* up with paid work too.

Today, *verynice*'s revenue streams look something like this:

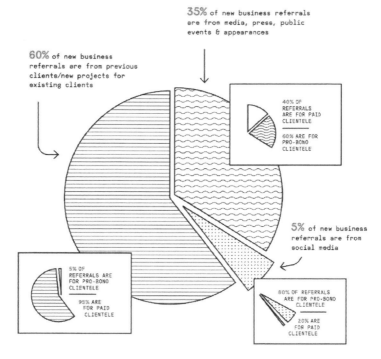

35% of new business referrals are from media, press, public events & appearances

60% of new business referrals are from previous clients/new projects for existing clients

40% OF REFERRALS ARE FOR PAID CLIENTELE

60% ARE FOR PRO-BONO CLIENTELE

5% of new business referrals are from social media

5% OF REFERRALS ARE FOR PRO-BONO CLIENTELE

95% ARE FOR PAID CLIENTELE

80% OF REFERRALS ARE FOR PRO-BONO CLIENTELE

20% ARE FOR PAID CLIENTELE

Fifty percent of the company's clientele is composed of 501c3 nonprofit organizations, and 50% is paid work (25% startups and small businesses, 20% for-profit social enterprises, and 5% Fortune 500 companies).

What started as an "impractical idea" solely operated by Manos has since grown into a team of 15 full-time employees – two business partners, a few managers, and a half-dozen vetted designers – all of whom oversee the work of 350+ volunteers and contractors around the world. The company has offices in Los Angeles, New York, and Austin.

And *verynice* isn't just a company – it's an ideology, a movement.

In October of 2013, Manos crowdfunded $10,000 to produce How to Give Half Your Work Away for Free, a book scrupulously breaking down the company's business model. A second version of his book, published just a few weeks ago and available for free online, has garnered attention from not just designers, but a wide array of business owners around the world wishing to integrate his philosophy.

Manos has lofty goals for the future. For one, he'd like to hit $10 million in pro-bono work by 2020 (*verynice* has currently given away about $1.5 million worth in services). Even more importantly, he'd like to scale the model he's created and provide small businesses with the means to replicate it.

"A lot of design firms optimize business to make as much money as possible," he says. "Obviously, making money isn't a bad thing – but what ultimately matters is the legacy our businesses leave behind."

So far, Manos's legacy is looking *very nice*.

THE LEATHER CRAFTSMAN

"This book ... is the culmination of over 30 years of knowledge and practical experience in Hand Sewing. It is presented to perpetuate the fading art of hand sewing in this age of mass production by machine."

– Al Stohlman
The Art of Hand Sewing Leather (1977)

When Andrew Diba saw the wallet – a beautiful, hand-crafted Japanese Red Moon – he fell in love. He longingly admired its contours and patina, and he imagined his fingers running across its expertly stitched edges. But a glimpse at the price tag soiled the recent high school graduate's fantasy: at $300, the wallet may as well have been on the moon.

Basking in the optimism of youth, he vowed to make the wallet himself.

First came the pangs of doubt: he lacked any artistic ability and possessed no particular penchant for design. His only experience with leather came a decade earlier, in the form of a 15-minute coin purse lesson imparted by a seamstress family friend. But Diba refused to be deterred.

His initial Google searches yielded little information on leather craftsmanship. There seemed to be only one definitive resource for such endeavors – a series of books from the 1970s, all written by one Al Stohlman, the apparent patriarch of leather craftsmanship. Armed with these dusty scripts, Diba embarked on a long, painstaking journey to master the craft.

By the time Diba had produced a wallet that satisfied him, he was a second-year university student. His new wallet was just as good as (if not even better than) the Red Moon he'd once desired. Several years later, he would start his own fine leather goods company, Neo Nouveau by Andrew Dibba, and become one of the few people in the world who practices the lost art of hand-stitching leather.

The Dark Arts of Leather Smarts

"To the beginner, Hand Sewing will seem uncomfortable and slow. Disregard all attempts at speed...learn to sew properly, as instructed."

– The Art of Hand Sewing Leather

Learning how to manipulate leather by hand is an ancient art form. For tens of thousands of years, clothing and shelter were made from animal skins. Left untreated, these skins would get extremely hard in cold temperatures and rot in warm weather. Over millenniums, humans realized that this could be avoided through the application of tannins from trees – a process called "tanning." The result? Leather.

Today, most expert knowledge of leather craftsmanship is either gone or difficult to access. As the vast majority of leather products – clothing, furniture, luggage, automotive seats – are stitched by machine, there is little interest in reverting to handmade techniques.

Hand crafting leather is also incredibly time-consuming and complex: producing just one stitch requires painstakingly piercing the leather with a metal awl and embarking on a series of loops and knots. It also entails navigating a myriad of decisions about which tools to use, which type of stitch to use, and how to cut the leather.

"You'll often encounter problems requiring a lot of experimentation," says Diba, as he recalls his grueling learning process.

Beyond The Art of Hand Sewing Leather, a sturdy 35-year-old manual written by Al Stohlman, Diba had little to go on when he first learned the ropes. Though a small number of leather artisans are still alive, they had no interest in sharing their wisdom with the young pup. Often, recalls Diba, he had no choice but to keep trying and failing:

> *"When I was learning, I emailed, I called. No one will train anyone. Either they don't want competition, or they want two years free apprentice. No one would train me, so I just trained myself.*
>
> *"I'd get stuck on things and figure it out through trial and error. I've done every-thing wrong at least once, so I can explain why I do it the way I do."*

On an online fashion industry website called Style Forum, Diba found respite. It was here, in the buried archives of forum discussions, that he came across a Hungarian shoemaker offering a month-long work-shop. In it, the apprentice would learn how to craft a pair of leather shoes by hand, and receive the man's expert guidance.

Diba saved up for months to afford the workshop's tuition, booked a flight, and flew to Budapest to meet him. Though he quickly decided shoemaking wasn't for him, he describes the experience of working with a real craftsman as life-changing:

> *"Most of the stuff I learned wasn't what I expected. It wasn't the actual skills, but rather the patience and how to understand the materials.*
>
> *I asked him, 'What do you want to do when you retire?' and he was like, 'What's that? I want to do this every day.' I thought, wow, this is what I want to do."*

Diba had arrived in Hungary with a vague interest in leather craftsmanship; a month later, when he boarded the plane, he felt a calling. "When you talk to a blacksmith or a wood worker, the material they work with speaks to them in some way," he tells us. "For me, it was leather."

Starting a Business

"You will find hand sewing is fun and easy. Speed will come by itself...with practice."

– The Art of Hand Sewing Leather

Diba started making basic leather belts, which are pretty simple: "Cut a strip, punch the slot for the buckle pin, punch a couple holes for the rivets, punch your belt holes, and cut the tip. It can be done in 20 minutes."

Soon, he began to wonder if he could sell his belts. On a whim, he sent an email, along with a few samples of his work, to a large department store. Management agreed to sell his goods.

Andrew Diba carefully crafts a handbag

Marketed under the store's brand name, Diba's belts sold quite well. But when the department store came to renew the contract and place an order for more belts, Diba declined. The belts were simple, lacked polish, and resembled other belts available in the market – and Diba dreamed of making masterpieces.

Instead, Diba kept his expenses low and worked odd jobs so he could practice:

*"It's crazy how much doing awful jobs
made me realize how much I enjoy
working with leather. I don't drink or
really go out much, and living in Victoria
British Columbia, [Canada], there are tons
of free things to do outdoors, so my expenses were, and are, really low."*

By the end of the year, Diba had designed a wallet,
belt, and briefcase – all of which were customizable and
met his standards. He wanted to sell his new wares, but
he had a problem: most fine leather suppliers demand
minimum orders of 500 square feet at $7 to $12 per
foot. Under these constraints, offering customers the
option of customizing the leather types would run Diba
thousands of dollars. After sending hundreds of emails,
he finally found overseas suppliers who specialized in
different leathers (calf, goat, kangaroo, and alligator)
and provided high quality leather with low minimum
orders.

With his product sorted out, Diba turned to finding
customers. Initially, he pursued the typical route of
selling to high-end retailers. But soon, Diba says, he
realized that "it was an awful idea":

*"There's a reason why there are no
Hermes-quality brands in high-end
department stores that aren't completely
vertically integrated like Hermes (as in
they own the tanneries, production, and
the stores themselves). After a store's
markup, my goods would be priced right
alongside luxury brands. While my quality
might have been better, you simply can't
compete with the brand name. That's why
nobody is doing it."*

When this failed to work, Diba got creative. He figured, why not sell the products directly to people who appreciate handmade leather products?

Going Viral on Reddit

In the months prior, Diba had acquired a large, gorgeous piece of alligator skin. He wanted to use it to create a briefcase that could show off the kinds of super-high-end pieces he could make for potential customers. While Diba painstakingly worked on the case, he took high-resolution photos of his piece. As an active member of the online community Reddit, he figured the photos would be a big hit there.

To accompany the images, Diba wrote a detailed, humorous, and accessible description of the entire process, which he casually titled, "Picked up some alligator and made a 5-figure briefcase by hand." With an optimistic click, he sent the entire thing into the vast digital strata of Reddit's "Male to Male Fashion Advice" sub-community.

Diba's posting became one of the most popular items ever posted to the "subreddit." Thousands of people endorsed its awesomeness by "upvoting" it. One floored commenter gushed:

> *"As a fellow leathercrafter, that handle modeling is fucking awesome. I've never seen it done that way before. Also can't believe you did that whole thing with a #10 blanchard. I did an iPad case in #10 and thought the stitching would never end!"*

Almost universally, Redditors commended Diba on the beauty of his product. "You got me," wrote one user. "I went from 'Why would anyone ever want a

$XX,XXX briefcase' to 'OMG I must have a $XX,XXX briefcase!'"

The Reddit posting generated over 100,000 views – exposure that instantly put Diba's business on the map. Major fashion magazines profiled him, organizers of important industry expositions invited him to present his collection, and droves of people visited his then-rudimentary website. At that point, the site didn't even offer the option of purchasing one of Diba's products.

Many people post their projects to Reddit, but very few of them cut through the noise and actually get noticed. This is especially true when people try to promote a business, a practice that some Reddit users frown on – even if the business is very cool.

One reason Andrew Diba's photo essay went viral is because it told a story. It showed Diba carefully examining the alligator skin, cutting the pieces, and deliberately hand stitching it. It chronicled the tiny details of his craft – glueing, waxing, cabling pieces together – and expanded on his thought process: Why did he design the handle a certain way? Why did he use a particular tool, or a particular method? It summarized, in one post, years of learning, toiling, and crafting.

After years of hard work and a fortuitous post to social media, Diba had finally accrued the customers he'd always wanted: people who appreciated handmade goods and were willing to shell out $300 for expertly crafted belts with a thousand stitches.

Neo Nouveau by Andrew Diba was born.

Today, running Neo Nouveau is Diba's full-time job. He is the only employee, spending half his time making products for his customers and the other half doing everything else: taking pictures of his products, writing descriptions for the website, procuring materials, shipping off the final product, and banal paper work.

His business isn't yet a huge success, but it makes money and Diba is proud of it. His goal is to get enough customers that he can spend all his time working on his products and hire employees to handle everything else. But for now, it's just Diba on his quest to make beautiful things made of leather.

NINA G:
THE STAND-UP WITH A STUTTER

Stand-up comedy is perhaps the most difficult form of public speaking. When a typical speech is not well received, the audience stops paying attention. But when stand-up comedians' punch lines fall flat, everyone can tell right away. No one laughs, and the room fills with a palpable, awkward silence. Sometimes a member of the audience yells "You suck!" at the comedian. This practice is called heckling, and it is generally considered acceptable audience behavior.

At the start of their careers, stand-up comics need to be either brave, confident, or delusional. But what if you stuttered? What if your entire life, teachers, classmates, and strangers grimaced when you spoke? Even if you dreamt of performing, would you pursue it?

Nina G stutters, and she's a pretty darn good stand-up comedian. She is fearless on stage, rattling off clever jokes, bantering with the audience, and all the while stuttering and pausing without a hint of self-consciousness. When we saw Nina G perform in San Francisco, it inspired a series of questions: Who is this person? Did she not get teased and bullied as a child? Did she not struggle with public speaking when she was younger? How did she come to embrace the ruthless world of stand-up comedy?

In software, there is an expression that goes, "That's not a bug. That's a feature." When the iPhone 4 was released, for example, Steve Jobs famously argued that its lack of Flash video support was a feature that ensured longer battery-life and fewer device crashes. A less optimistic person might have called it a bug, since most of the web's videos were in the Flash format at the time.

Nina, who is the world's only female stand-up comedian with a stutter, embraced a neurological condition and owned it as part of her comedy product. She took what some might call a limitation (stuttering) and turned it into the foundation of her comedy career.

What It's like to Stutter as a Kid

When Nina performs onstage, she exudes self-confidence. That wasn't always the case. Nina wanted to be a stand-up comedian ever since she was a little kid, but she didn't work up the nerve to do it until her mid-thirties. She explains:

> *"I wanted to be a comedian since I was 11 years old, but I didn't really think of it seriously since I stuttered and that wasn't something that comedians did. I remember from being a little kid just loving comedy. Steve Martin, Saturday Night Live. I loved it.*
>
> *Anytime I had to do a book report, it was about comedy. In college, whenever I could, I'd write papers analyzing stand-up comedians and their impact. Whenever I had free time as an adult, I'd go watch live comedy. I always just loved comedy."*

Nina grew up in Alameda, California, a suburb of San Francisco. When she was eight years old, she started stuttering. Around the same time, she was diagnosed with a learning disability. Compared to her learning disability, she says, stuttering actually wasn't a big deal:

> *"Going to Catholic school with a learning disability was the big problem. The school was so set in its ways, they wouldn't do anything to accommodate me unless my parents fought for it.*
>
> *When I started stuttering at the age of eight, it was no big deal for my parents. My Dad had a hearing impairment; my Mom's mom had polio. This was just something that happened, part of life. They were always really supportive."*

Nina's parents didn't think of her stuttering as a problem to be fixed. It was just a part of life. Nina's childhood speech therapist was also a great source of support, helping her learn how to communicate more effectively without treating her stutter as a personal flaw.

Four percent of children stutter, but only one percent of adults stutter. For some people, stuttering goes away as they get older. Others have it for life. Many fall on a continuum in between.

Nina recalls the first time she stuttered in front of a large public audience:

> *"I remember in 7th grade I was in the student government, and during the 'inauguration,' you had to say your name in front of the whole school. I practiced and practiced so I could say my name without stuttering. But then, on the day of the inauguration, I couldn't say my name.*

I just stuttered in front of the whole school instead of saying my name. Afterwards, I was sure everyone would laugh at me.

But you know what? People didn't laugh at me. Afterwards a girl came up to me and said, 'Nice job Nina.' I thought at first she was being sarcastic, but then I realized she really meant it.

There was one exception. Right afterwards, I was hanging out with a friend of mine, this 8th grader. A second grade boy came up to me and said, 'Hi n-n-n-n-Nina.'

My friend the 8th grader got down on one knee to look the 2nd grader in the eye and told him 'If you ever say that again, I'm going to tell the whole school you have a tiny dick.'"

To Nina, the consequences of stuttering in front of the entire school were relatively minor. People didn't seem to mind. Instead, she discovered the value of having an "advocate" who "had her back," whether that advocate was fluent or stuttered. Sometimes when you have a disability, you just need someone to defend you, even if that means berating a second-grader.

Howard Stern: Disability Advocate

As a teenager, Nina accepted stuttering as part of her life that might not go away. She did so with the help of an unlikely role model: an actor on The Howard Stern Show. Watching Stern's outrageous, low-brow radio and television show, Nina saw someone in the media "stutter openly" for the first time:

> *"Howard Stern was the only show I ever*
> *watched where one of the main characters*
> *stuttered. Stuttering John was a part of*
> *the show. They made fun of him like every-*
> *one else and he wasn't treated any differ-*
> *ently on the show because he stuttered. He*
> *was the first person I ever saw on TV that*
> *was just stuttering openly.*
>
> *Stuttering John would go around inter-*
> *viewing celebrities and it was really inter-*
> *esting to see how people reacted to him. I*
> *was fascinated by what assholes people*
> *were. Chevy Chase once told him, 'Maybe*
> *if someone hit you, you'd stop stuttering.' I*
> *still hate Chevy Chase because of that."*

Nina had wanted to be a comedian since she was 11, but she didn't regard it as a realistic goal. Comedy and television were places for people who spoke fluently, not for someone like her:

> *"I didn't think I could be a comedian be-*
> *cause I stuttered. There was no one on TV*
> *who stuttered unless it was a 'very special*
> *episode' with a character that had a prob-*
> *lem because they stuttered.*
>
> *You just get the message that comedy is*
> *not the place for you. TV was a place for*
> *fluent people."*

Instead, Nina focused her energy on working as an advocate for disability rights, driven by her experiences growing up. Nina remembers one issue she faced because of her disability:

> *"It's the teachers who treated me badly*
> *that I blame, because they had the power. I*
> *did a presentation with a friend in school*
> *and my friend got an A and I got an A-*
> *because I 'didn't speak clearly.' Of course I*
> *didn't speak clearly. I stutter, you*
> *[redacted]!"*

Nina attended community college and then transferred to UC Berkeley. She later earned a graduate degree and became a full-time advocate for people with disabilities. For the next decade, she spread the message that those with disabilities are okay the way they are – it's society that needs to fix itself by better accommodating those with disabilities.

Middle Age Regrets

Nina entered her mid-thirties feeling like she'd simultaneously accomplished a lot and not enough. On one hand, she had a successful career advocating for individuals with disabilities. At the same time, she still dreamt of being a comedian, and she had never given that dream a shot.

Often, Nina would tell herself she was "doing pretty well for someone with a disability." But even though she had dedicated her life to empowering the disabled, stuttering became her excuse to be timid. So as not to subject others to her stutter, she spoke up less often than she would have liked, and she was a much meeker person than she is today:

> *"I was comfortable in my own skin, but I*
> *still let my disability limit me. I wouldn't*

*talk as much as I would otherwise, so I
wouldn't make other people uncomfortable. I would be in relationships that
weren't always good for me because of self
esteem issues I carried around from stuttering and my learning disability. I was in
a state like, 'I'm doing pretty well in life for
someone with a disability,' but I was still
letting my issues around my disabilities
limit me."*

Everything changed in 2008 when Nina attended
the annual conference for the National Stuttering
Association, which she hadn't attended since she was a
teenager. Nina describes attending this conference as a
turning point in her life:

*"Being around all these people that
stuttered, I realized how differently I was
acting back at home. I was afraid of
'taking up too much space' by subjecting
people to hearing me talk. I was being
meek and small, and I didn't realize it until
I was around all these other people who
stuttered and I was able to be myself.*

*It was a four-day conference, but by the
end, I was changed."*

When Nina came home from the conference, she
immediately severed ties to the people in her life who
had made her feel like she should act meek because of
her disability.

She also enrolled in a stand-up comedy class. Nina
had decided that her stutter was not an excuse. She
would finally pursue her dream of being a comedian.

Making it in Stand-Up Comedy

The odds of "making it" in the stand-up comedy circuit are slim. According to San Francisco comedians we spoke with, the last household name that emerged from the local comedy scene was Dana Carvey, and that happened two decades ago.

It's not only difficult to become famous, it's nearly impossible to make a living wage.

Almost all stand-up comics start their careers by going to "open mics." Anyone can perform, but audiences are generally small. Open mics are a good way for stand-up comedians to improve and gain stage experience, but they don't pay.

Short sets that last five to ten minutes and pay $10 to $50 are one step up from open mics. Promoters hire several comedians for these shows, rent a venue, and sell tickets. Some comics, if they spend about a decade building their network (so people connect them with these gigs) and working on their material (so their gigs go well), can string together enough paid shows to earn a living wage. But most don't. During this process, a few comics are "discovered" and end up with their own TV show as the next Louis CK. That is extremely rare.

In 2012, a *New York Times* feature investigated the finances of stand-up comedians. The "beginner" stand-up comedian profiled in the article earns $2,500 a year from comedy and makes her living as a receptionist. The comedy "veterans" in the article, who have ten or more years experience as performers, make between $65,000 and $85,000 a year. They make a living, but they have to hustle for it – they perform on cruise ships, sell CDs, and find voice gigs and podcast sponsors.

An experienced comedian, Eugene Mirman, represents the top of the pyramid. He makes $200,000 a year by headlining large comedy venues and earning regular TV credits. But as he's not a household name, he considers his current success tenuous. "There's no one thing that 'makes' anybody unless you're on a hit show that has your face on it," he explains, "and even then, however famous or successful anyone gets, it can all go away."

Nina G Takes the Stage

In February of 2009, Nina dove headfirst into standup comedy. Her first experience onstage was validating. "The first time I performed, it's not like I was amazing," she says. "But it was like, 'Ah, this is right for me.'"

Stand-up comedy is a difficult craft to master. If you spend an evening at BrainWash, a San Francisco laundromat that doubles as an open mic stage (and triples as a cafe and bar), you'll notice that most of the performers are still trying to figure out how to be funny on stage. You'll also notice that comedians waiting for their turn to perform make up most of the audience.

Nina performed at a show in San Francisco, Berkeley, or Oakland almost every night after work. After a few months, Nina landed her first paying gig, which paid $10. That first year, she sunk almost a thousand hours into practicing, writing, and driving to comedy shows that generated only a few hundred dollars in total revenue.

In many ways, stuttering is an asset for Nina onstage. When you see Nina at a show, you remember it, because you've likely never heard a performer tell a joke about what it's like to stutter. This helps her stand out in the sea of male performers talking about their comic books, horrible day jobs, and crappy love lives.

When we ask Nina if stand-up comedy is particularly challenging because she stutters, Nina demurs. Stand-up comedy is hard for everyone, she tells us, but she does have to deal with a few challenges that other comedians don't.

For starters, many audience members don't know whether it's okay to laugh. (It is.) They worry that it's making fun of Nina's disability to laugh at her jokes about stuttering. (It is not.)

Others think Nina fakes her stutter. These people literally can't believe that someone who stutters is a stand-up comedian. Nina's YouTube page frequently has comments from viewers accusing her of being an impostor. As Nina has said onstage, she never fakes: "I have a rule that I don't fake my stuttering and I don't fake my orgasms."

Nina G. in her element

Finally, Nina's stutter can throw off her comedic timing. Jokes generally have a set up, followed by a snappy conclusion called the punch line. If the punch line isn't delivered with the right timing – if it's delayed by Nina's stutter, for example – it can fall flat, even if the joke is well written. To account for that, Nina writes her jokes with a particular structure so that the joke will be funny even if the timing on the punch line is slightly off.

Nina has turned her experiences as someone who stutters into some of her best jokes. A guy she met at a bar who told her to "spit out" her name when she stumbled over it is now the butt of one of her mainstay jokes. When someone asked her why she couldn't stop stuttering "like that King's Speech guy," she wrote a routine about which parts of the movie were accurate and which were not. It's funny, but also informative.

Nina has embraced the educational aspect of her comedy. She started touring with a group of comedians with disabilities on the "Comedians with Disabilities Act." They travel the country and perform in front of much larger audiences than Nina gets at a typical show in San Francisco. She's also started putting on disability training seminars for companies that mix comedy and corporate training. She sells shirts at her shows and recently self-published a children's book about accommodating disabilities.

Although Nina earns some money as a comedian, it's hard to make a living from performing. Nina performs about 25 shows a month, but she only gets paid for one or two of them. Recently she performed in Memphis, Tennessee, and she made $800. But she had to pay for her own plane ticket, so she only netted $200. Despite her growing commercial prospects, Nina will make only a few thousand dollars from stand-up comedy this year. She still has her day job as a disability advocate.

In one of Nina's sets, she tells the story of a comedy club manager who told Nina that if she kept practicing and doing opening mics, one day she'd finally have the "self-confidence" to stop stuttering.

Nina's response to the manager crystallizes her story perfectly:

"If you get up on stage and you stutter, then maybe self-esteem isn't your frickin' issue...plus, if I stopped stuttering, I wouldn't have an act. So let's hope that doesn't happen."

We all have characteristics that mark us as different. When you're a kid, that can mean being bullied or told your dreams are out of reach. Even if no one tells us that explicitly, we may get that idea – maybe from watching TV and noticing that no one on the screen looks or talks like us. As a result, we may have regrets later on in life about the paths we never pursued.

As a child, Nina got the message that she couldn't become a stand-up comedian because she stuttered. But one day, she decided to ignore that message. She tried stand-up comedy, and she was good at it. She channelled her differences into a unique perspective. While every other comedian makes jokes about male genitalia, Nina makes jokes about male genitalia and social justice. If Nina makes it big as a stand-up comic one day, that "and" will have made all the difference.

THE CHOCOLATE HACKER

Jonas Ketterle "discovered" chocolate the summer after quitting his job as a mechanical engineer and product designer. He and his girlfriend were traveling through Mexico, nursing each other out of an episode of Montezuma's revenge, when a textile artisan invited them to camp in his courtyard in a village about an hour outside of town. They took him up on it.

One afternoon their hostess, the artisan's wife, introduced the couple to her family, and the grandmother asked them if they'd ever made chocolate.

"The second she'd heard we hadn't," Ketterle says, "she ran into the stock room to get the cacao beans."

In the shadow of a sacred mountain, she showed the two travelers how to roast the beans on a pan over an open fire, moving them around with a brush. "It's actually very difficult to roast cacao over a fire," Ketterle tells us. "She was very good at it." The heat dried the beans' papery outer husks, which the three spent "several hours" shucking by hand. They then ground the beans into a paste using the village's stone grinder and sweetened it with local honey.

As you might expect, Ketterle had eaten chocolate before, but not chocolate like this. The pair carried the chocolates with them on the rest of their trip, sharing them with the people they met. "People loved it. It was the best chocolate I had eaten up to that point," Ketterle says. "I remember thinking, 'Wow, I made this with my hands.'"

When he returned to the United States, Ketterle says he became "obsessed" with figuring out how he could make chocolate from home. "I had just moved to North Carolina with my partner, and I had decided to take a little time to figure out what my next step would be," Ketterle chuckles. "But if there's one thing I've learned about myself, it's that I never really take a vacation."

Days would turn into nights, the North Carolina fireflies would come out, and Ketterle would still be in the kitchen, tasting chocolate, tweaking his recipe, and taking notes. He quickly dispensed with pan-roasting and hand-shucking. He hacked together his own specialized equipment, and what he couldn't build he bought with money he made through part-time work designing and building alternative energy products. He started logging his recipes and their variations, and he slowly developed an engineer's understanding of the variables that contribute to chocolate's texture and flavors: the origins of the ingredients, their balance with one another, the method of grinding the beans, the darkness of the roast, the temperature of the chocolate in its liquid form, how long it was stirred, and how quickly and with what.

Pretty soon, Ketterle had made more chocolate than he knew what to do with. But he did know one thing – he wanted to make even more, and he wanted to make it better. To do that, he needed some fancier equipment and a real kitchen. Jonas Ketterle decided to make the plunge into the world of chocolate-making and launch a company, Firefly Chocolate.

A Willy Wonka for the Modern World

Jonas Ketterle's curly brown hair hangs down past his shoulders. Outside of chocolate, he's mostly worked for startups that bring alternative energy technologies to developing regions. He takes long walks in redwood forests, does yoga, and drinks green smoothies. He now lives in an ecovillage in Sebastopol, California, where some of his neighbors herd goats for dairy and sheep for wool. He is known amongst friends to take breaks from whatever he's doing to close his eyes, smile, and breathe deeply, appreciating the moment.

If you were to infer that, in addition to being a traveler, engineer, and chocolatier, Ketterle is a bit of a hippie, you'd be right.

Jonas Ketterle husking cocoa beans in Mexico

"Cacao is fundamentally a plant-medicine," Ketterle says. He's partially referring to the wealth of research on chocolate's health benefits. The consumption of dark chocolate is correlated with a lower Body Mass Index (BMI), lower blood pressure, lower cholesterol, and higher serotonin levels. But he also points out that the latinate name for chocolate – theobroma cacao – literally means "food of the gods." How, Ketterle asks, could the experience of eating it not be sacred?

This attitude is reflected in Firefly's company mission statement: "Inspire awe and wonder." It's also reflected in his recipe. While the sweeteners in most chocolate offset the benefits of the cacao, Firefly's chocolate recipe never dips below a ratio of 85% cacao bean solids – in the standard nomenclature, this means it's 85% dark chocolate. It's also vegan, soy-free, and sweetened with coconut sugar, which Ketterle says is both healthier and more sustainable than cane sugar. Firefly purchases the cacao beans whole, from a farm in Belize that Ketterle describes as the market's moral "gold standard."

Ketterle's recipe and attitude ensure that Firefly fits right into the "craft chocolate movement." The movement consists of small-scale chocolatiers who manufacture chocolate from scratch ingredients, and it has grown enough to challenge Big Chocolate, the large candy companies that add sweeteners to chocolate and source cacao beans from morally questionable places.

Jonas and the Chocolate Hackery

When he made his first batch of chocolate in his home kitchen, Ketterle says he found most everything he needed online – and not just cacao beans, which most grocery stores don't stock. He found a community of chocolatiers who were overwhelmingly generous with their tips, tricks, and recipes. He's since become deeply involved in the craft chocolate movement, and he says that he fits right in as an engineer.

"When we get together, one of the things we say a lot is, 'Oh yeah, I modified that machine in that way,'" Ketterle says. According to him, there are few trade secrets, and he's trying to make Firefly's operations as transparent as possible. "We're trying to grow craft chocolate as a movement that can compete with industrial chocolate. We're all massively supporting each other in an ecosystem of chocolatiers, rather than thinking of each other as competition."

There are a few basic steps to making chocolate from a cacao bean: 1) roasting the beans, 2) removing their husks, 3) grinding them into liquor, 4) "conching" that liquor (stirring/kneading the heated liquor for anywhere from hours to days to improve flavor and viscosity), 5) tempering it, 6) pouring it into molds, 7) waiting for the mold to cool.

According to online tutorials, an aspiring home chocolatier can carefully roast his beans in a toaster oven (Step 1), husk them by hand (Step 2), and mold them in whatever he wants (Step 6). All the other steps are trickier. For example, Step 3: liquefying the dry roasted beans. This is done by releasing and then heating the cacao butter fats inside the beans. One tutorial recommends sending the beans through a juicer several times. The tutorial's author adds:

If your juicer doesn't generate enough heat (i.e., nothing comes through the juice port), have [a] friend point a hair drier at the auger end of the juicer until everything starts melting and flowing smoothly. Be careful not to blow all your cacao away with the hair drier as it comes out of the juicer (I've learned this from experience).

Another would-be chocolatier notes that a coffee grinder can be used instead, but results in a "sandy mouthfeel." Reading that, it's not surprising that the first piece of equipment Ketterle bought was a stone-grinder, which achieves a very fine grind and heats the butter through friction alone.

"A lot of chocolate equipment has become more accessible," Ketterle says, "as more and more people start making chocolate. But some stuff you still need to make yourself."

As he made more and more chocolate, the hand-made process Ketterle learned on his trip through Mexico became less and less practical. Ketterle realized that there was probably a better way. Industrial chocolate processors roughly chop the beans with the husks still on, and then use a mechanical winnower to whisk away the husks, which are lighter, from the cacao bean chunks called "nibs." These machines are too big to fit into most kitchens – even most commercial ones – and, Ketterle says, can easily run $10,000. So Ketterle followed the advice of the online community of craft chocolatiers and built his own out of plastic plumbing and a vacuum cleaner.

"Custom built machinery always takes a lot of fine-tuning," Ketterle says. "I cut into the vacuum cleaner's power cord and hooked up a $10 speed controller I got on eBay." When the controller is calibrated exactly right, the husks are whisked up by the airstream and the nibs drop to the bottom. When it's calibrated wrong, Ketterle either ends up with husks in his nibs or nibs in his vacuum cleaner.

As he made even more chocolate, Ketterle decided he needed even better equipment. And he faced a question: to build or to buy?

Chocolatiering is a very delicate process with a long history, and Ketterle felt like he couldn't personally improve on the state-of-the-art machinery in many of the steps. "The technology is pretty mature," he says. "My old machines were basically operated by on-off switch, and these new ones allow extreme precision, which makes a difference."

"But the field is rapidly evolving in other areas," he adds, "and there are certain stages of the process where I can do something just as good myself."

The practice of making chocolate from the bean, as opposed to from liquor, is less established, and the technology is less developed. Which is why Ketterle is keeping his winnower: now the very same vacuum cleaner and speed controller are hooked up to a beautiful, custom-blown glass tube. But many of the other sophisticated pieces of machinery Ketterle wanted, he decided he was going to have to buy. And to do that, he needed money.

Crowdfunding Confection

Ketterle's new machines would allow him be more precise with his chocolatiering, and also more efficient. With his old machinery, he made about 10 pounds of chocolate per batch, which is about 60 bars. With the new machines, he could make about 100 pounds of chocolate at a time, or 600 bars.

"That's still small in the world of commercial chocolate," Ketterle says, "but in that quantity, it was going to make sense to start selling it." This is how he decided he needed a company – because he wouldn't be able to sell chocolate otherwise. When he registered Firefly, chocolate wasn't yet approved as a "cottage food" in California, which meant he couldn't have legally sold it out of his home kitchen. Even though the law has since changed, Ketterle is glad he decided to incorporate. Had he gotten cottage food certification, and then decided to scale up to 100-pound batches, he would have had to face many of the same hurdles later.

The fact that Ketterle couldn't legally sell chocolate out of his home, however, meant he couldn't fund his access to a commercial kitchen with chocolate sales. So he turned to crowdfunding. He made a campaign on the fundraising platform Tilt (formerly Crowdtilt), and he let funders pre-order chocolate as a reward. "To sell food to the public, you have to do it out of a certified facility," Ketterle says. "I was crowdfunding in order to get the equipment and pay for that facility."

To promote his crowdfunding campaign, he also brought free chocolate samples to conferences, farmers markets, and friends' living rooms – so people would know what he was asking them to fund. While Ketterle was experimenting with his chocolate recipe and production process, he knew the free samples had to represent his product at its best. Nobody wants to fund a company that make shitty chocolate.

Firefly chocolate is, in the author's experience, very tasty – extremely dark and not particularly sweet, but also not particularly bitter. It has an unusually soft, fatty texture and rich, complex flavor. Many a potential funder took the time to savor it. And while they savored, Ketterle pitched.

Apparently a good time to ask for money is when someone is eating chocolate – Firefly's month-long campaign raised $10,040. With those funds, Ketterle has begun remodeling a commercial kitchen and aims to deliver rewards to his funders in February of 2015.

And when it came to starting a company, Ketterle had a secret weapon: he actually seemed to know what he was doing.

"I've been working in startups for years," Ketterle explains, "but never at the helm. This was a great opportunity to start something myself." He had thought through per-unit economics for packaging. He had considered how many employees he'd need and how to go about hiring them. He knew exactly which machines he wanted and how much they would cost. Chocolate was his passion, sure, but he had the discipline to approach the business side of Firefly as a real business.

Ketterle says he got much more than money out of campaigning for funds to start his company. He found the immediate gratification of watching people taste and enjoy his chocolate intoxicating. "Most of my work experience has been in international markets, impacting people thousands of miles away from where I live," Ketterle says. "Chocolate has a more local impact on my own community."

AMERICA'S FIRST
NOT-FOR-PROFIT BAR

Everyone has an excuse to buy one more round of drinks, but here's a new one: it's for charity.

The Oregon Public House bills itself as "the world's first non-profit pub." Patrons approaching the Portland pub pass a sign that reads "Have a Pint, Change the World," and the pub has three menus, one for food, one for beer, and one for local charities that receive 100% of the bar's profits. Diners and imbibers can choose which charity they want to receive the surplus from their bill.

The pub has raised over $15,000 for charity since it opened its doors last May, and it plans to donate more once it's better established. According to Ryan Saari, founder of the Oregon Public House, the goal is to donate $10,000 a month – an aspiration that will call for business savvy as well as generosity. "We want to be the most profitable nonprofit," he tells us.

A nonprofit bar may sound like an "only in Portland" phenomenon, but the Oregon Public House has peers in the Okra Charity Saloon in Houston, Shebeen in Melbourne, and, until recently, Cause in Washington D.C.

Despite its nonprofit status, the Oregon Public House doesn't enjoy much in the way of tax breaks. And that's the way its founders like it. "We are trying to set a model that doesn't need special privileges," says Saari. "We want to show that we can run a successful business but at the same time give back."

The bar is an intensely local product of a city with a craft brewing craze and a state with a strong nonprofit sector. Yet it also aspires to further a global ambition – to marry commerce and charity, profits and good works. A nonprofit bar may sound like a punchline, but its backers are serious about showing that Adam Smith's invisible hand can be a bit more generous.

Liquid Fundraising

A night of beer and wings at the Oregon Public House is not a sanctimonious experience. Other than its family friendly vibe, the pub feels much like any other bar. "It's just a fun place to have beer and connect with friends," Saari tells us. Board member Stephen Green adds:

> *Many people come without knowing about our mission. We have three different signs: eat, drink, and give. And people are perplexed by the last one [until] we explain.*

You don't overhear many conversations about charity in your average watering hole. But in Portland's "philanthropub," it's a common occurrence as patrons decide which charity to donate the proceeds of their meal to. Both Green and Saari love when customers first learn that their order supports charity – that "Wow. Duh!" moment, as Green calls it, when people realize that they don't have to choose between spending money on a night out or supporting charity. Saari explains:

> *My favorite thing is sitting at the bar, having a drink, and listening to people place an order. The bartender asks, 'What*

*charity do you want that to go to?' And
they say, 'What?' It's amazing to see that
spark as they find out what's going on."*

That spark first came to Saari four years ago at a barbecue.

As Saari sat in his backyard, barbecuing with friends, the group discussed how to get involved in the community. As Saari related to The Oregonian, they knew that Portland was saturated with nonprofits. But every nonprofit needed help fundraising. Saari suggested a pub.

For those wondering who runs the world's first nonprofit bar, the answer is a team of volunteers led by the coolest pastor you know. Ryan Saari has done charity work with the homeless and for AIDS causes, and he has worked on community outreach in schools. He is also the pastor of a church that The Oregonian describes as follows: "Indie music plays over speakers and pews are replaced by candlelit tables where patrons sip coffee during the sermon."

Several years after Saari and his friends first debated the idea in his backyard, the pub is now a reality, and it has the community aspect the friends imagined. As patrons debate which organization (out of the rotating group of local nonprofits) to donate the proceeds from their check to, they discuss the local challenges those charities tackle. Friends of the Children, for example, partners vulnerable children with a professional mentor from kindergarten through high school graduation. My Voice Music gets youth involved in musical programs, and Habitat for Humanity builds affordable housing. The charitable aspect also brings in a slightly wider clientele, as supporters of the nonprofits come in for meals. "We get some non-pubgoers," Saari tells us.

The pub has started functioning as the "fundraising department" for Portland's nonprofits that Saari imagined. It donates all its monthly profits or "surplus" – about $1 of a $5 local beer is profit, while margins on food are thinner. Saari hopes to start an in-house brewery, with different beers each supporting a different cause. So, as the *New York Times* noted in an article on the pub, customers buying Oregon Public House Education Ale "would know the proceeds were going to an education charity supported by the pub."

New philanthropubs like the Oregon Public House, while not plentiful, are a new model, distinct from Whole Foods donating 5% of its sales on "5% days" or Toms donating a pair of shoes to a child in need with every purchase. Yet it is also a democratized version of a staple of the fundraising playbook: the charity gala.

Whether it's to raise funds for anti-trafficking programs, a local school, or the Met, $1,000 per plate galas raise millions of dollars each year for charitable causes. The per plate price is a donation, as well as a ticket to an exclusive party where attendees can mingle with celebrities, network with business associates, and enjoy high society – all at a discount thanks to charitable tax deductions.

In a sense, the Oregon Public House is the middle class gala, allowing anyone to turn a night out into charity without the allure of celebrities and without nonprofits turning into entertainment companies for the night. And the government doesn't even subsidize the bill: despite its nonprofit status, the Oregon Public House pays its taxes.

A Profitable Nonprofit

The leadership of the Oregon Public House hopes that they will inspire others to copy their model. But they don't recommend going the nonprofit route.

"We wanted the credibility that comes with nonprofit status," Saari tells us, noting that the pub's books are publicly available so that customers can see that he and the other board members are volunteers who don't make a dime off the bar. "It's a cynical society, and we wanted to be above reproach." The state of Oregon recognizes the bar as a nonprofit, but the IRS does not. Saari says that the federal government kept asking for precedence, and they kept responding that they were the first of their kind. He believes that the concern that the Oregon Public House would have an unfair advantage over other establishments sunk their application. A suggested donation model may have worked, but the board worried about people donating a dime for a beer. So they decided to pay their taxes.

The result was a lot of extra paperwork that limits some of the business practices available to the pub (due to their state-recognized nonprofit status) without the tax advantages of national nonprofit status. "Just one of those things you learn," Stephen Green reflects.

Yet the board wasn't disappointed with the outcome.

The partial nonprofit status earns the bar a lot of trust, and the seeming incongruence of a "not for profit pub" attracted media attention from the *New York Times*, *NPR*, and *The Colbert Report*. (An irate Stephen Colbert warned that beer and charity don't mix, and worried that he might wake up the next morning asking, "Ugh, who did I feed and clothe last night?")

Nearby businesses and breweries are supporters of the Oregon Public House. "We buy a lot of our beer from them," says Green. "We help make the area a destination." That support may have been strained if the Oregon Public House entered the same business tax-free.

The pub's board is particularly pleased with their status because it gives them the opportunity to prove a model. To show that a business can survive and thrive with charitable giving as its mission. "We want to show that we can run a successful business but at the same time give back," Saari tells us. He enjoys the Oregon Public House's community aspect, but he points out that businesses from t-shirt shops to tech giants could orient themselves around the goal of fundraising charitable ventures.

Despite being a nonprofit, profitability is the bar's number one concern. The food industry has a notoriously high failure rate, and even successful brewpubs spend years paying off the upfront costs of establishing a restaurant. The other reason the bar's owners prioritize profits, just like any business, is that it means they can donate more to charities.

For this reason, while the staff is paid, the pub's board draws no salaries. "Our goal is to donate $10,000 a month, and we need to be lean and mean to do so," Saari explains. "Managers not drawing salary is a way to do that." Bottom line concerns also explain why it took so long for the pub to go from concept to reality. Instead of taking out loans, the bar's founders relied on donations. After three years of fundraising $100,000 and receiving around $150,000 in donated materials and labor, two other philanthropubs had opened before the Oregon Public House.

Not that it's a problem for Saari, who is "excited for others to steal this model" and says, "We don't care if we're the first or the coolest. We want to be the most profitable nonprofit and give over $100,000 a year to other nonprofits." Thanks to their lean practices, there are encouraging signs. The Oregon Public House has donated over $15,000 to charity since it opened and earned at least one ranking as top brewpub in Portland.

Model Capitalists

As the Oregon Public House has gained renown around town, Ryan Saari and Stephen Green have started talking to other Portland businesses about acting as fundraisers for nonprofits. None have so far copied the Oregon Public House in donating 100% of their profits. Green talked with a furniture company, for example, that is considering donating a fixed percentage of profits from select items.

Skeptical customers may question whether business owners are actually more interested in using charitable donations to draw in customers than to support the work of nonprofits. But the cut and dry practice of donating funds sidesteps charges of greenwashing or using a disingenuous commitment to a social cause as a marketing ploy. Green tells us that "there's definitely a cache, being in Portland" to supporting social causes, but he believes that nonprofits will appreciate the money regardless of the business owner's intentions.

Beyond Portland, the work of the Oregon Public House fits into a broader movement working to free business from the limitations of a purely profit-maximizing mindset.

Today, 34 states and the District of Columbia have either passed or introduced legislation that allows new companies to register as "benefit corporations" – a form of incorporation, Stephen Green notes, that the Oregon Public House would have pursued if it had been legal in Oregon at the time of the pub's founding.

In classic corporations, executives and board members feel bound by the widely accepted (if legally disputed) concept that they must maximize value for their shareholders and investors, with value defined in strictly monetary terms. In benefit corporations, however, board members pledge to pursue both profits and social good.

Momentum in the movement to marry commerce and ethics can also be seen in the growth of socially responsible investing, which now represents "one out of every nine dollars under professional management in the United States." The catchall term for any attempt to invest in order to maximize financial return as well as social good, it includes strategies from refusing to invest in sin industries like smoking and gambling to focusing on socially and environmentally focused companies.

Both Saari and Green are bullish on the prospect of business working for social causes and charitable giving. Describing businesses interested in donating proceeds to attract customers, Saari tells us, "They still want to do some good." Green, meanwhile, cites the book Drive, in which writer Daniel Pink argues that people are less motivated by money than they are by the opportunity for "autonomy, mastery, and purpose."

Green reflects that "a lot of the businesses [that we are working with] have a passion for what they do. And they need to make a living. But people do lots of things where there is no financial incentive." He and Saari are chief examples, as they receive no compensation for serving on the pub's board other than the satisfaction of being involved in their community.

A nonprofit bar seems very much the product of Portland's cause conscious, craft brew loving, think local culture. The backers of the Oregon Public House, though, look forward to a time when mixing work, volunteerism, and social causes is the norm. Until then, people can at least raise money for Portland's charities, pint by pint.

THE UNDERGROUND ECONOMY
OF DOLORES PARK

A parade of half-naked hunks dressed like Jesus, a six-foot mylar robot dancing to techno music (who you now know as Robot Dance Party), a grandfather hula hooping in a leopard-print man thong: these are the characters who inhabit Dolores Park. On any given sunny weekend in San Francisco, ten thousand people flock to the palm-laden park in the city's Mission District.

Over the last few decades, Dolores Park has morphed into a minimally-regulated free space: vendors peddle goods, drug dealers conspicuously sling product, and Mission denizens fearlessly sip cans of beer in public. On the last Sunday of every month, the park celebrates this free-spirit attitude by hosting the Really Really Free Market, where "nothing is bought and nothing is sold." People bring all kinds of stuff – from highchairs to Titanic-sized sweatpants – and take what they need.

The park is a paradigm of free-market capitalism. Vendors roam openly beneath Mexican fan palms, selling goods to the needy masses. For weed smokers and PBR drinkers, Dolores is the Elysian Fields; police presence is sparse and the goods are plentiful.

The park presents a healthy challenge to the cliche that conservatives love free markets and liberals embrace regulation: capitalism seems to suit San Francisco's hipsters just fine.

A Brief History of Dolores Park

Coined "Hipster Hill" by locals, Dolores Park has a history even deeper than your v-neck.

The land was inhabited by Ohlone Native Americans for several centuries, divided by the Spanish when they arrived in 1776, and later taken over by prospectors during the Gold Rush. In 1861, a synagogue, Congregation Sherith Israel, purchased the space and used it as a Jewish cemetery; over 1,900 bodies were buried on the plot before it closed in 1894.

After a decade of neglect, the city purchased the land for $293,000 ($7.7 million in 2014 dollars) with the goal of creating "one of the most beautiful parks to adorn San Francisco." A 1905 article from the San Francisco Call laid out elaborate plans for the new space – a man-made lake, a track, a gymnasium, semi-tropical plants – but before construction could start, tragedy struck.

In 1906, a magnitude-7.8 earthquake destroyed 80% of San Francisco and killed more than 3,000 people. The city converted Dolores Park into a refugee camp, and it remained one until 1908. According to a historic evaluation of the park, the camp included "512 three-room houses for 1,600 refugees" and cost the city $74,000; the displaced paid rent to stay there.

Though the park was developed a few years later, it wasn't until after World War II, when an influx of Latin American immigrants settled in the surrounding Mission neighborhood, that Dolores Park became a cultural hotspot. In the late 1960s, as hippies flocked to the city, the park developed a reputation as a hub for drug use; by the 1990s, it had become a go-to location for transactions. With the arrival of this new culture, a free market sprung up in the park – and not just for drugs.

A Laissez-Faire Zone for Vendors?

Despite its "chill" facade, Dolores Park is a laissez-faire marketplace and bastion of free-market capitalism.

Ever since the city built a playground in the park in 2009, surrounding communities have lobbied for a more family-friendly park; as such, there has been more of a concerted effort to curb illegal distribution. Yet while some vendors have been cited and had their wares seized, most seem to have continued business as usual.

The "Truffle Guy" is among the lucky: he is unquestionably a Dolores Park staple. Toting a trademark straw hat and an array of copper pots, he has gained a cult following as a (supposed) weed chocolatier. His golf-ball-sized treats come in six flavors – coconut, espresso, cinnamon, ginger, pecan, and mocha – and customers can buy three for $10 or seven for $20. The Truffle Guy says "one is usually enough for the average person."

Also known as Trevor, he is itinerant and has an unpredictable schedule. Some weekends, he's out in full force, and other weekends, he's nowhere to be seen. But on the days he ventures out, he does well for himself. A source who claims to know Trevor well tells us the chocolate prince sells 120 truffles on a good day, securing $400 to $500 in revenue.

His fan-produced Yelp page boasts 64 reviews and a 4.5 star average rating – higher (figuratively and literally) than some Michelin-rated restaurants. Online, his customers furiously debate whether or not his products are actually "enhanced." One user claims, "half an hour in, I tripped so hard I ripped my pants." But another contests, "total duds...where's the beef?"

The Truffle Guy has many competitors, including local gangs who sling in the park, and, until recently, the "Ganja Treat Man." Dolores Park dilettantes regularly heard his sales call, "Have no fear, the real ganja man is here!" until the Ganja Man's arrest and citation in 2012. Witnesses say they saw plainclothes cops stop the vendor, question him, and take him away in cuffs, his trademark wizard cane in tow.

The "Costco Pizza Man" tails the Truffle Guy and cashes in on weed-induced munchies. He merely buys four Costco pizzas for $9.95 a pop and sells them for $4 per slice. Accounting for his $40 overhead, with ten slices per pizza, the Costco Pizza Man makes away with a quick $120 profit over an hour or two. (His slices tend to sell quickly.) Rumor has it that before he slung pizza, he sold beer out of paper bags; following police warnings, he changed his business model.

Selling beer in Dolores is certainly not a novel idea. For years, a man named James, more lovingly known as "Cold Beer, Cold Water," sold cold beer and cold water. Known for distributing PBR for a markup (two cans for $5), CBCW often filled his small cooler with three 12-packs (purchased for $15 each at a corner store) and sold out within 20 minutes. He'd then return and repeat the cycle. Over a few hours, according to Uptown Almanac, he would make $200 to $300.

The police arrested CBCW in 2012, during a crackdown, and forbid his alcohol sales. CBCW continued to sell water bottles, but his profits significantly dwindled.

"Hey Cookie!" is a goddess among baked-goods connoisseurs. Pigtailed and wearing any of her 25 milkmaid-esque dresses, she circulates Dolores Park on the weekends, selling an amalgam of (non-laced) cookies. She says "some people are put off to be offered a non-medicinal treat in the park," but she has thrived. She sells a long list of treats – paleo coconut cups, gluten-free, rich chocolate morsels, snickerdoodles, vegan mexican wedding cookies. While she hesitates to discuss profit, she has accrued regular business outside of the park's confines, often selling at local bars and to companies including Apple, Twitter, and Ubisoft.

"Hey, Cookie!" and her delicious baked goods are a fixture at San Francisco's Dolores Park

Another treat called paletas (Mexican ice cream bars) are plentiful in the park, but one man, Hector, says he has an edge over competing vendors: he's been selling his coconut-flavored bars in Dolores Park since 1990. Over nearly 25 years, he's learned the hot spots and has developed a natural intuition for seeking out high-demand environments. He doesn't solely sell his pops in Dolores, but he says that "on a good weather Saturday, it's the best place to make money."

When he first started out, Hector purchased his paletas wholesale from Delicias de Jalisco for $0.42 each, and he'd sell between 75 and 100 fruit bars a day at $0.75 each, which net him about $30 on an average day. Business hasn't improved much over the years. Today, he gets his bars from La Michocana at $0.65 a piece, and he sells each one for $1.50; on a good day in Dolores, he sells 100 bars and brings in $68.

But popsicle sales are especially dependent on good weather; on mildly rainy, windy, or otherwise chilly days in the park, Hector's sales drastically decline. When the weather is bad enough to keep hacky-sacking aficionados indoors, Hector doesn't even bother selling. It's his only source of income, and it's a tough life – the hours are brutally long, he's on his feet all day, and his makeshift cart creaks and wobbles like a 90-year-old's kneecap – but he persists and chips away at making an honest living.

***

You'd never know it from experiencing a Saturday in Dolores Park, but a rigorous set of rules and regulations in the San Francisco Municipal Code delineate acceptable behavior in the city's parks.

Smoking and public drinking is prohibited, and vending food or alcohol is strictly illegal. Add the city's general prohibitions to the mix – peddling without a permit, marijuana possession (albeit as the San Francisco police department's lowest priority) – and it's a wonder that Dolores Park continues to function as it does.

The city has made several efforts to crack down on illegal activities in the park. In 2012, the police handed out 17 citations to vendors in just a two-month span; in 2013, the city imposed a curfew on hanging out in Dolores Park and closed the park between the hours of 10pm and 6am. But still, laws of any sort seem to be very sparsely enforced: hipsters continue to drink, stoners continue to blaze, and vendors continue to sell goods, largely without any hassle from the police.

So is Dolores Park truly a free market economy? Not entirely – but it's probably as close as you can get in America. The forces of supply and demand are minimally impacted by laws and regulations; goods are sold at freely-set prices, adjusted based on supply and demand. The vendors are more often at the mercy of sunny skies and generous crowds than legislation and police.

By most accounts, Dolores is a capitalist's utopia, and both the vendors and their clientele intend to keep it that way.

THE FOUNDING OF HACKER SCHOOL

"This sounds like a crazy plan for a startup, I realize, but this is the right sort of crazy...if it doesn't make money, it will at least have been a benevolent thing to do."

– Paul Graham, co-founder of Y Combinator, on Hacker School

Several times a year, dozens of computer programmers leave their jobs, put their lives on hold, and move to New York City for three months to enroll in Hacker School. There, they focus on one thing: getting better at writing code.

There are no teachers, no classes, and no formal curriculum. Instead, the programmers improve by working together on real world, "open-source" computing projects that they release for others to freely use. With no other distractions, they practice coding.

If this doesn't sound idyllic to you, you might not be the target audience for Hacker School; the people who attend Hacker School absolutely love it. Not only do they get to work with cool people and improve their skills, but they don't pay any tuition – Hacker School is free. Instead, the school makes money when talent-starved tech companies pay headhunting fees to recruit its graduates.

Since opening its doors in 2011, Hacker School has made a name for itself in the technology world. Many of the program's visiting "residents" are luminaries in their fields, companies endow grants to cover the living expenses of its female and underrepresented minority applicants, and over 500 programmers have graduated from the program since it started. Hacker School has quickly made a sizable impact on programming education.

And yet for the school's founders – David Albert, Nicholas Bergson-Shilcock, and Sonali Sridhar – it probably feels as if it has taken a long time. Their path to founding Hacker School was riddled with false starts, rejection by investors, and the cardinal sin of startups – making products that no one wanted.

***

Nicholas and David met in an undergraduate computer science course at Columbia University. Though David was the type of person who always arrives last and Nicholas the type who always arrives first, the two became close friends and discovered that they worked well together. Nicholas and David agreed that some day, when the timing was right, they'd start a company together.

After graduating in 2008, the two friends worked as programmers for different companies in New York City. In their respective workplaces, they each observed the difficulty of finding and hiring good programmers. After collaborating, they came up with what they deemed a great solution: a questionnaire that programmers could answer about their skills and interests, which would then be used to match them with employers. In 2010, Nicholas and Dave quit their jobs to work on the idea full-time.

They didn't know much about how to start a company, but the two figured they needed to create a business plan. Not knowing how to do that either, they stumbled upon an application form which asked helpful questions like "What will your company make?" and "Who are your competitors?"

The form came from Y Combinator, an extremely competitive, Silicon Valley-based "startup incubator" program that provides young companies with funding, advice, and valuable connections. Since its inception in 2005, it has hatched some of the biggest technology companies in the world. Since Nicholas and David had already used Y Combinator's form to write their business plan, they decided to hit "submit" and actually apply. They beat out thousands of other applicants to earn one of only 34 spots in the program.

In the summer of 2010, Nicholas and David packed their bags to move to Silicon Valley and participate in Y Combinator. During a three month tenure spent building their company, they met Brian Chesky, a Y Combinator alumnus who ran a then-small but fast growing startup called Airbnb. Brian became a mentor to the company.

Early on, Brian suggested that applicants who used Nicholas and David's product should be able to submit video responses to questions. They took the advice and made video interviews a centerpiece of the software. Nicholas and David named their company "HireHive," and TechCrunch, a widely-read tech industry blog, covered their public launch.

As the YC program progressed, however, the pair realized that what they built wasn't working. They saw some traction among companies using the software to screen salespeople and customer support professionals, but none of these companies used it to hire programmers. Programmers, they discovered, hated making videos of themselves answering questions.

The duo's Y Combinator program culminated with Demo Day, a high-stakes series of presentations in which founders pitch Silicon Valley's top investors for money. Most of the companies raised millions of dollars in seed funding for their technology startups. Nicholas and David did not. Every single investor who they spoke to rejected HireHive.

After their unsuccessful fundraising process, the duo decided to pull the plug on HireHive. It may have worked in some non-technical industries, they surmised, but it would have required a staggering amount of work, and their hearts wouldn't have been in it. They didn't want to make it easier to hire sales reps – they wanted to make it easier to hire programmers.

"We entered a shockingly long period where we made the same mistake over and over again," recalls Nicholas. "We made software that no one needed." The two created a search engine for finding people based on their skills, and they attempted a few more prototypes vaguely related to the task of hiring programmers. None of their ideas gained traction, although they did manage to recruit Sonali, a designer who Nicholas had previously worked with, to join the team as a third founder.

Floundering, the team turned to Y Combinator's partners for advice. Paul Graham, Y Combinator's leader at the time, offered a suggestion: Instead of imagining what software recruiters need to hire programmers, you should just become recruiters yourselves. As recruiters, Graham continued, David, Nick, and Sonali could then build the software that they needed.

So, the team launched a head-hunting firm that they called "Hackruiter" – a recruitment and placement agency for programmers, by programmers. Per the recruiting industry standard, the company would collect $20,000 whenever it referred a programmer to a company that hired him or her. Before launching, they secured a small amount of seed capital from two prominent investment firms: Founder Collective and SV Angel.

Quite a few companies signed up for Hackruiter. After all, signing up was free, and companies only had to pay a bounty when they made a hire. But companies were only half of the "connecting employers to programmers" equation: Hackruiter still needed programmers.

To counterbalance this, the team spent almost 100% of their time trying to meet talented programmers. They went to meetups, set up coffee meetings, and sent strangers emails asking if they wanted a new job. The founders each went to 12-15 meetings a day, which was incredibly time consuming and not much fun. Moreover, it didn't help them come up with better product ideas. They still didn't know how software could help companies hire great programmers. In fact, they started to doubt whether software could solve the problem at all.

"It became clearer and clearer that the challenge was not in writing the software to match people, but in finding good people," says Nicholas. "It was a supply problem."

Not only was there a very limited supply of qualified computer programmers in the world, but within that pool, almost no one knew about Hackruiter. The company fished in a small pond, and it didn't have good bait.

The trio needed to address the shortage – by increasing the number of qualified programmers in the world – and get that talent to come to them. Clearly, matching software wasn't the answer. Marketing the recruiting firm as "run by programmers" wouldn't work either. So, the team rethought their approach.

They returned to an idea that they had mulled over

since they started HireHive: the creation of a university specifically for programmers. The founders had always treated the idea as a pie-in-the-sky sort of fantasy – one they would indulge down the line, when their successful software startup could fund a new university. The idea wasn't for a traditional school exactly, but more of an "unschool" where people could learn programming by working on interesting projects.

They began to wonder if a school had been the right approach all along. Creating a place where people could become better programmers would certainly increase the world's supply of programming talent. Moreover, a good school (or a good "unschool") would be a honeypot for good programmers: it would attract driven and intellectually curious people, make them even better programmers, and send them into the workforce – possibly even through Hackruiter.

The idea excited the founders, but after bouncing from idea to idea, they had started to doubt themselves. Why couldn't they see an idea through? Were they quitters? Were they just not tenacious enough for the startup scene? Hackruiter wasn't a booming recruitment firm, but they had made some placements. They earned $20,000 in revenue about every other month, which covered costs, and if they focused on the service, that number would certainly grow.

But the idea for Hacker School kept gnawing at them: what if it were a good idea? Similar institutions existed for other crafts. If a poet or a novelist wanted to focus on a project, for instance, she applied for a creative writing fellowship or a writer's workshop, where she would receive mentorship from faculty and commune with peers over a shared craft. There should be something like that for programmers, the team reasoned – a place to share and celebrate the art of code. Nicholas recalls their dilemma:

"We were excited about the idea, but we were skeptical about it because we had already pivoted so many times. We wondered: Are we being erratic and should we be stubborn and work on [Hackruiter] and make it work? In retrospect [Hacker School] was a good idea, but at the time, it wasn't clear to us at all."

In the end, we decided to try an experiment to see if this model had any legs. If we could get space [for the classroom] for five weeks, and find five people to commit to it, we thought we'd be able to determine if the idea had real promise."

***

The team set out to discover if programmers would drop everything for five full weeks, just to develop their skills and work on open source projects.

After Sonali secured a New York University classroom, the team reached out to the network of people they met through Hackruiter with a pitch:

"Here's this thing we've been thinking about that will be a 'writer's retreat for programming.' We'll work on open source projects, it won't be about startups. It will just be five weeks to become better programmers."

After a few weeks, nine people committed. Three of them dropped out two days before the session began, but the founders still surpassed their goal of five people. Moreover, Nicholas, David, and Sonali decided to participate. Nicholas explains:

"We didn't feel like we were good enough programmers to teach people, so we wanted something like [Hacker School] so we could get better at programming. From the start, we would be just as much students as anyone else. Sure, we had some other commitments like administering the program and running Hackruiter, but we were there to learn too."

The team made several policy decisions focused on making Hacker School an environment conducive to self-directed learning. They decided the program should be free, so they could attract programmers who were passionate about self-improvement, regardless of whether they could pay. The program would also focus on real open-source projects, instead of artificial classroom assignments. In order to avoid the "get rich quick" attitude that pervaded other tech environments, the founders also made explicit that Hacker School was not a startup incubator. It would be a pure haven for programming.

Most importantly, they set up specific community norms to make Hacker School a good place to learn. In the first batch of participants, there was just one social rule: "no saying 'well-actually'" to demonstrate how smart you are by correcting someone:

"A well-actually happens when someone says something that's almost – but not entirely – correct, and you say, 'well, actually...' and then give a minor correction. This is especially annoying when the correction has no bearing on the actual conversation."

The first session of Hacker School was a smash success: participants loved the program and felt like they had improved at programming. By the session's end, people were chatting nostalgically about the "good old days" when they first started Hacker School, five weeks prior. As Nicholas put it, "It was the first thing we built that people loved."

Though the program was free, Hacker School got paid. At the end of the five week program, they placed one of the participants at a company through Hackruiter. The $20,000 headhunting fee paid for the program's expenses and demonstrated that the company's business model could work.

***

The success of Hacker School's pilot program relieved its founders. They had finally created something people actually wanted, and they could shutter their recruiting firm and end the drudgery of sitting in meetings all day. They dedicated themselves to Hacker School, confident in the decision to pivot to their new idea.

For the second run, they lengthened the program from five weeks to three months. Spotify, the music streaming company, agreed to provide them with free office space for the session. This time, they managed to recruit 12 people to participate. Hacker School had already doubled in size.

By the third batch, they were ready to publicly launch Hacker School. When they submitted their launch announcement to Hacker News, a web forum popular with programmers, the response was astounding. One mid-career programmer wrote:

> *"The idea of spending three months full-*
> *time in the company of like-minded souls,*
> *building cool stuff with new technologies*

*and learning together is practically
orgasmic for someone like me. (I know,
I'm pathetic.) This would be the
opportunity to "catch up" in all the things
I've been wanting to do in an intense, three
month period."*

From there, Hacker School began its steady, linear rise. Famous programmers started attending the program as residents, batches got bigger and more frequent, and the founders instituted more community rules to make it an even safer learning environment. To help address the lack of women and minorities in the technology industry, Etsy, an e-commerce company, started endowing grants to cover the living expenses of female and minority programmers who were accepted into the program. Other companies followed suit. Graduates of the program evolved into a passionate alumni community that wanted to see the program thrive. Hacker School started achieving its goal – to increase the supply of great programmers in the world.

Today, even as programmers clamor to attend Hacker School, and despite advisors suggesting the founders start charging tuition, the program remains free. Hacker School kept placing graduates through its recruiting program, which brought in revenues that helped fund a growing staff. The team has swelled to eight full-time employees.

Hacker School is now "a thing" in the programming community, and well en route to becoming an institution. Over 200 programmers went through the program this year alone – and 500 since the school's inception three years ago. If it continues to grow at this pace, it will soon graduate more programmers each year than the most prestigious universities in the world.

***

Despite its success, Hacker School's position is tenuous. Unlike a university, the company has no endowment or tuition. In any given batch, the number of graduates they place with companies that pay a referral fee varies greatly. In turn, the company's revenues fluctuate wildly. If Hacker School doesn't work hard at placing its graduates at partner companies, it risks running out of money and disappearing.

Although the founders participated in the first sessions of Hacker School, today they spend less time coding and more time building the company. Nicholas barely gets to code at all, he says, because he has to focus on the business side of Hacker School and ensure they have enough money to thrive.

More money means more staff and resources; more staff and resources means more people can attend Hacker School; more Hacker School graduates means more talented programmers in the world. If they can pull off the business model, Hacker School's founders will have created a durable, self-sustaining institution. If they can't pull it off, everything they worked so hard to achieve could all just go away.

Such is the pressure startup founders face as they try to make a mark on the world.

THE BUSINESS OF PHISH

Over the past four years, the rock band Phish has generated over $120 million in ticket sales, handily surpassing better-known artists like Radiohead, The Black Keys, and One Direction. Since their start 30 years ago, Phish has consistently been one of the most popular and profitable touring acts in America, generating well over a quarter billion dollars in ticket sales.

Yet, by other measures, the band isn't popular at all. Only one of their original albums has ever made the Billboard top 10 rankings, and none of their 883 songs has ever become a popular hit on the radio. They've made only one music video to promote a song, and it was mocked mercilessly by Beavis and Butthead on MTV.

If the traditional business model for a rock band is to generate hype through the media and radio airplay, and then monetize that hype through album sales and tours, Phish doesn't fit the model at all. For a band of their stature, their album sales are miniscule and radio airplay non-existent. As a result, when the "music business" cratered in the 1990s because of file-sharing and radio's importance declined because of the Internet, Phish remained unaffected and profitable as ever.

Phish doesn't make money by selling music. They make money by selling live music, and that, it turns out, is a more durable business model. Neither the band nor its managers pre-calculated this business model; it just emerged as the natural consequence of the kind of music Phish makes. The band developed the kernel of this musical style during their first five years, when they played almost exclusively in bars in Burlington, Vermont, and slowly, but organically, grew their audience.

During this period Phish maniacally focused on improving the quality of their music through intense practice and frequent gigs. At first these gigs were relatively unsuccessful, but over time, their audiences grew, the band started to make money, and then, after five years of obscurity, they were profitable before anyone in the music industry knew who the hell they were. With profitability came the freedom to make music on their terms.

In the parlance of startup language, Phish bootstrapped their business rather than seeking support from institutional players like record labels, talent agencies, and concert promoters. And that's made all the difference.

10,000 Hours of Jamming

Phish got their start in 1983 at the University of Vermont (UVM) where Trey Anastasio, Jon Fishman, and Mike Gordon were all students. Page McConnell, a student at nearby Goddard College, joined the band two years later. Since then, they've been the band's core: Anastasio on lead vocals and guitar, Gordon on bass guitar, Fishman on the drums, and McConnell on keyboard/piano.

In his 2008 book Outliers, Malcolm Gladwell popularized the 10,000 hours theory of human genius. The theory posits that natural talent is a necessary, but not sufficient condition for achieving greatness in a given field. An aspiring genius must put in thousands of hours of "deliberate practice" to achieve virtuosic status in fields ranging from software development (Bill Gates) to physics (Robert Oppenheimer).

The band Phish exemplifies this theory that deliberate practice at an early age leads to "outlier" performance. Anastasio, the band's frontman, started playing the guitar at the age of seven and performed in serious bands by middle school. Fishman, the drummer, started playing at the age of five. McConnell started playing the piano at the age of four. By the time they entered college, not only were they accomplished musicians, but they were united by their preference for practicing music over attending class.

From the band's early days until the late 1990s, they showed a near fanatical obsession with practice. In a Phish biography, Fishman, the drummer, remembers college as follows:

> *"Basically I locked myself in a room for three years and played drums and went to band practice."*

Gordon, the bassist, relates an eight-hour, chemically-assisted practice session that was not atypical:

> *"Trey used to take fresh chocolate and vanilla and maple syrup and all these natural ingredients and make four small cups of hot chocolate that had a half-ounce of pot in them... [So] we started this jam session and it ended up going for eight hours."*

Even as the band became popular a decade later, they continued to practice intensely. Sometimes they engaged in highly analytical listening exercises. Phish biographer Parke Puterbaugh explains one of these exercises:

> *"The best known was called 'Including Your Own Hey.' These exercises, which formed a large part of their practice regimen from 1990 through 1995, are not so easy to explain but important for understanding how Phish could maintain a seemingly telepathic chemistry in concert.*
>
> *"Hey" means we're locked in,' explained Anastasio. 'The idea is don't play anything complicated; just pick a hole and fill it.' They explored different elements of music —tempo, timbre, dynamics, harmonics— within the 'hey' regimen."*

While today Phish is well known as a "jam band" that improvises on stage, it wasn't until 1993, ten years after their formation, that the band really unveiled this skill. According to the band archivist Kevin Shapiro:

> *"Before 1993, it had seemed to be a very practiced, concise show that flowed real fast and didn't necessarily have any huge improv moments. All of a sudden there were huge improv moments everywhere."*

Before Phish achieved success, they worked hard at their craft. At the peak of their success, they practiced just as hard, if not harder. Later, they abandoned these regular practice sessions, which could either be seen as a cause or a symptom of the problems that led to the band's breakup in 2004.

The Slow, Linear Rise of Phish

"Burlington is an excellent womb for a band. It's relatively easy to get a gig, you get paid decently, and it's not a cut-throat situation at all."

– Jon Fishman, Drummer of Phish

Before the band had even settled on a name, Phish played its first gig at an ROTC Ball in late 1983. If you've heard Phish play, you know that their music probably wasn't the best choice for future army officers and their dates to boogie to. Eventually, the band was drowned out when someone put on Michael Jackson's "Thriller," and the evening was resurrected – from the ball attendees' perspective at least.

After a brief detour when lead singer Anastasio was suspended from UVM for sending a human heart and hand through the U.S. Postal Service as a prank, most of the band transferred to Goddard College where they could pursue a self-directed study of music. During this period, they started to regularly play gigs at local bars.

Phish's first regular bar gig was weekdays at 5pm. Their friends made up most of the small audience. After the ROTC dance debacle, they couldn't even get booked for campus gigs, let alone real music venues. But they stuck with playing bars at off-peak hours and eventually the audience swelled modestly from their friends to their friends and friends of friends. Phish biographer Parke Puterbaugh comments:

> *"This all worked to Phish's advantage, as they weren't swamped by success but experienced a slow, steady climb, during which they nurtured their craft in an environment where they gained a following one fan at a time. They*

gradually cultivated a varied audience of
college students and hipsters from
Burlington and environs."

At this time, Phish started to display the organic growth in their fanbase that characterized the rest of their careers. They won over fans one at a time through their live performances, and those fans recruited their friends to come to the next show.

Eventually, a more popular local bar called Nectar's invited Phish to play. At Nectar's, they moved from the the upstairs stage to the main stage. In the Phish biography, band frontman Anastasio remembers:

> *"Usually there wouldn't be that many*
> *people at the beginning of the night. People*
> *would come and go, and it would just kind*
> *of swell. Eventually, it started getting*
> *really packed, which is why we had to stop*
> *playing there. But for a long time, it*
> *wasn't."*

Eventually Phish started to get a lot of stage time at the more popular bars in Vermont. During this time, they honed what would become their signature talent – keeping a live audience enthralled, dancing, and having fun all night. Fishman describes the freedom to experiment they enjoyed during this time:

> *"For five years we had Nectar's and other*
> *places around town to play from nine until*
> *two in the morning... We'd get three-night*
> *stands, so we didn't even have to move our*
> *equipment. Basically, the crowd was our*
> *guinea pig. We'd have up to five hours to*
> *do whatever the hell we wanted."*

In the same Phish biography, Tom Baggott, a Phish fan and acquaintance, reminisces about what it was like to hear Phish in those days:

> *"They sort of sucked when we first started seeing them... They were getting it together. They were sort of sloppy, you know, but that was the fun of it. That was the magic of it. It was like there was a big joke going on and all the early Phish fans knew the punch line—which was that this was gonna be something big."*

These insanely loyal fans not only dragged their friends to shows, but also started taping the shows and passing out the tapes to friends. Rather than squelch this "piracy," the band encouraged it. The tapes provided great marketing that led to greater show attendance, and it helped develop an obsessive fanbase that would later want to collect everything Phish: rare recordings, concert experiences, official albums, and merchandise.

After years of honing their craft on their homecourt of Burlington, Vermont, Phish got their big break in 1989. Or rather, they manufactured their big break. The Paradise Night Club, a 650-seat venue in Boston that served as a proving ground for rock bands, refused to book Phish. By this time, Phish had two buddies working as their business managers and booking gigs. The managers took a gamble – they rented out The Paradise and assumed the risk of selling the tickets themselves.

With the help of their now diehard fans, Phish sold out all 650 seats. Many of their fans trekked down from Burlington. One fan organized two buses from Burlington that, together, brought almost one hundred fans. The rabid fan base that Phish had cultivated from its five years of gigging in Burlington paid off big time.

Selling out The Paradise opened a lot of doors for Phish. Phish biographer Parke Puterbaugh relates the scene in the Boston music industry:

> *"Beth Montuori Rowles recalled the reac-*
> *tion at Don Law's office the next day:*
> *'Jody Goodman, who was the club booker*
> *at the time, was like, "Does anybody know*
> *who this band Phish is? They sold out The*
> *Paradise last night. How did that happen?*
> *I've never even heard of them before.*
> *They're from Vermont. What is this? They*
> *sold the place out!"'*

All of a sudden it was like the radar's on them. The next time Phish played in Boston, the Don Law Company promoted it. They wanted a piece of it. End of story."

Phish started touring in progressively larger venues. Still, the growth was never exponential or Bieber-esque. In an interview with High Times, Anastasio reflects:

> *"If you look at the whole 17 years of Phish,*
> *it was an exact, angular rise. It was at the*
> *point where our manager used to be able*
> *to predict how many tickets we were going*
> *to sell in a given town based on how many*
> *times we had played there previously.*
> *Every time we played, it got a little bit*
> *bigger, and it kept getting a little bit*
> *bigger."*

Shortly after selling out The Paradise, despite not a single music label or management company knowing their name, the band became profitable. Rather than rush to put out a Top 40 hit, the band could focus on doing more of what was already earning them money: making music and touring.

Number of Phish Shows Per Year

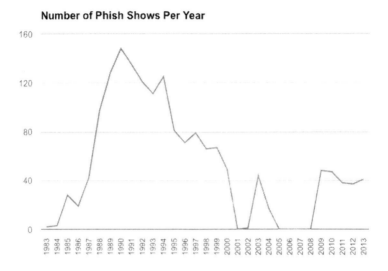

From then on, the band rapidly accelerated their touring, performing well over one hundred times a year all over the country.

By the end of 1994, they sold out the Boston Garden for a New Year's Eve show. The run cemented Phish's status as a big time band that could sell out arenas, bring tens of thousands of fans to remote weekend festivals, and generate tens of millions of dollars in ticket sales per year.

They were bona fide rock stars.

Why Do People Like Phish?

So what type of music did Phish learn to play in Burlington, Vermont, that inspired such a loyal following? Among people who don't frequently listen to

Phish, the band's popularity can be baffling. But if you spend any time watching videos of the band's live performances on YouTube, you'll see masses of enthusiastic fans hanging on the band's every note and raucously dancing around.

Why do people love Phish? Partly because the band is comprised of immensely skilled musicians. After years of intense practice, not only are their individual skills strong, but as a collective entity, they know how to play with each other. But this can't be the whole story: they may be skilled performers, but listeners disdain virtuoso musicians every day. The band's technical skill alone cannot explain their popularity.

Another part of the answer is that Phish's live performances are built around interaction. That's the product that Phish sells: the interplay between the band and audience. The audience is an integral part of the show.

When the audience hears the right cue from the guitar, the fans know to chant "Wilson," and they know that Wilson is the antagonist from Anastasio's senior thesis, an epic musical composition. When the song "You Enjoy Myself" comes on, the audience roars with delight when the guitarists jam while jumping on trampolines, even though they know it's coming. As you listen to live recordings of Phish, you notice that for every note the band plays, the audience provides a response that guides the band. It's the back and forth between the audience and the band that creates the live musical production.

If going to a U2 concert is like purchasing a mass-produced print, a Phish show is like buying a unique painting. The band has never played the same set list twice, and you never know when a ten minute song could morph into a thirty minute improvised jam.

Fans don't merely go see Phish; they collect Phish experiences. They track the number of concerts they've gone to, which songs from the band's catalogue they've heard, and which venues they still need to see Phish perform at. Due to the band's improvised and varied sets, Phish fans constantly collect new experiences. Popular shows like Gamehoist, Big Cypress, Clifford Ball, and Salt Lake City 1998 have taken on near mythological proportions.

So while Phish is a rock band and an interactive experience, the band has also created an immersive fantasy world that fans can get lost in, not unlike The Lord of the Rings, Star Wars, or Game of Thrones. There is a mythology about the band – and its songs and shows and history. Just as a fan of Lord of the Rings may memorize Frodo's family tree, a Phish fan knows all about Gamehendge (the fantasy world setting of many Phish songs) and Rhombus (it's complicated).

Finally, Phish puts a lot into each show. The band might fly through an arena playing on a giant hot dog, play an eight hour set till sunrise, or pretend that Tom Hanks is on stage with them. There is a whimsy and unpredictability to their shows. The drummer occasionally plays a vacuum cleaner onstage, and he almost always wears a woman's dress while performing (except when he performs naked). At any Phish show, something strange, amazing, or unique could happen. For the diehard fan, the fear of missing out on one of these shows drives them to try to attend every one.

All of these reasons for why people do like Phish also explain why other people don't like Phish.

Almost none of the experience of watching Phish live translates over to their recorded music. Their studio recorded albums, without the excitement and energy of the audience, sound comparatively sad and lonely – almost like the difference between eating a great meal with a group of friends versus all by yourself. Same food, different experience. And while the music may demonstrate technical prowess, the complicated, layered, 30-minute jams performed by the band don't translate well to the radio.

Some people in this world love Phish more than you can possibly understand. This author's wife is one of those people, and this author is not. As a compromise, one Phish song was played during the dancing portion of this author's wedding reception. When that song came on, half the dance floor cleared out. They stood to the side and stared with befuddlement as the other half of the attendees danced to a slow, strange, and seemingly undanceable song. The Phish fans were in rapture. Their favorite band was blasting through the speakers, and they knew that if "Tweezer" was performed now, then "Tweezer Reprise" would make an appearance at the after party.

The Business Model

Beginning in 1989, before the band had even signed a record deal, Phish was profitable from live touring. That profitability only came after five years spent scraping by on gigs in Burlington's bars, but during that time, they developed their most valuable asset: the ability to enthrall fans through live music.

Because Phish achieved financial independence before the music industry even recognized them, they could more or less do whatever they wanted. They used that freedom to develop complete control over both the artistic and business aspects of their music.

The band took their early profits and started their own management company, Dionysian Productions. They hired a staff of over 40 people that handled their elaborate stage productions and back office operations. They built their own merchandise company so that their shirts and other paraphernalia reflected the band's artistic sensibilities. They even started a mail-order ticket company so that fans could send them money orders and buy tickets directly from the band.

In 1991, Phish signed with a major record label, Elektra, which is owned by Warner. As they had the leverage in the relationship, Phish never really had a lot of conflict with their label about artistic control. They didn't need money from album sales, because they made money from live shows. So they never had to dilute their artistic vision to get radio airplay and sell albums. Of course, the result of this artistic freedom was that they never sold albums at a rate commensurate with their popularity.

Perhaps more so than any major musical artist today, the Phish business model is derived from having hard core fans of its live music. When Madonna sells out arenas across the country, she's selling tickets to her various fans that live everywhere. When Phish sells out arenas or festivals across the country, it's because the same die-hard fans fly across the country to see the band. In the rare instances where fans don't make the trek and the shows don't sell out, the band punishes the no-shows by performing a particularly epic set. In an online forum where ardent Phish fans compare how much money they spend going to see the band, the answers are in the tens of thousands of dollars.

So while Phish undoubtedly has fewer fans than Madonna, the ticket revenue per fan is much higher because fans loyally attend multiple shows. Not since the Grateful Dead has a band built a following as loyal as Phish. And like the Grateful Dead, Phish merchandising is a big business as fans gobble up Phish t-shirts, baby-onesies, and hats.

When file sharing and piracy ravaged the music industry, Phish was insulated because their primary business was selling access to live music, not recorded music. In fact, the band took advantage of the trends of digital downloads and streaming. They bundled digital downloads of live performances with ticket sales so that everyone who attended a show could download its broadcast the next day. And those who can't attend shows live can pay to stream the performance from Phish's website. While technological advancements have made it harder for some artists to profit from their work, if anything, it made it easier for Phish to do so.

The Rise and Fall and Rise of Phish

In 2004, Phish broke up. Fan speculation centered around several reasons: rampant drug use by the band, the financial pressure of having over 40 people on payroll who needed to be paid whether the band toured or not, or that after more than 20 years of a grueling tour schedule, the band had simply run its course.

In an interview with Charlie Rose right after the breakup, frontman Anastasio gave a compelling reason for the breakup – the passion for making great music together was no longer there. Anastasio tells Rose how he once felt about the music:

> *"You know, it was like — the only thought was about the show. I mean, I used to lock myself in my hotel room as soon as the concert was over. For years, I would run back to my hotel room and start working on the set for the next night. And even though there wasn't really a set list, there kind of was. Like, I knew what was going on. And I was working and working and working, you know, oh my God, for hours, ripping pieces of paper up, books, you know. And then hours before the show, songs we hadn't played in a while — I mean, it was just like a heavy work ethic until we got on stage. And then it was just a celebration."*

The band that practiced so diligently for most of its tenure stopped practicing together in 1998. By 2004, fans began commenting that the musical quality of the band was declining. What could have been a triumphant final show in Coventry, Vermont, was a disaster. Rain and mud wreaked havoc on the weekend, and the band's musical performance was universally panned. The musical geniuses of Phish went out with a whimper.

Phish Inc started to become a more bloated, drug-polluted entity precisely as their desire to make great music together waned. It was time to call it quits.

Until, that is, it was time to call it un-quits. The band reunited in 2009 for a three-night show in Hampton, Virginia. The announcement sent a shockwave through the Phish community and an even greater shockwave through the Ticketmaster ordering system; the heavy traffic crashed the site. In the five years since the breakup, the band had cleaned up, streamlined their staff, and rebuilt the personal relationships between the band members. And so, in a testament to the strength of the following they built, they reunited and have generated over $120 million in the subsequent years.

Our Intent Is All For Your Delight

The members of Phish knew they wanted to make music since they were little kids, and they worked at it harder than anyone else. They have generated hundreds of millions of dollars in concert sales, but their roots were humble and their growth was slow. They spent five years in the relative obscurity of Burlington, Vermont, perfecting their craft. And through that process, they learned how to entertain a live audience. That turned out to make all the difference.

Every time Phish played, their audience grew only slightly. But devoted fans evangelized their music and the word spread. Growth was slow, but it compounded until suddenly the band could sell out 650 seats. And then one day they could sell out Madison Square Garden four nights in a row. And some of those fans attended the show all four nights, and the ones who didn't wished they had.

Phish worked long and hard to become great musicians and performers. This has led to a durable business model built around live concerts. Could another band replicate their success? Maybe. But how many of them would quit before realizing how good they could be? Or be discovered by the music industry too early and release a major label record that flops?

At a Phish show in 2003, the crowd was greeted by a giant banner proclaiming, "Our Intent Is All for Your Delight." It's Phish's pure devotion to music that makes them beloved of their fans. It's also what ended up making them gob fulls of money, so that worked out nicely.

CITATIONS

Introduction: Consider the Hipster

Hipster (Merriam Webster):
http://www.merriam-webster.com/dictionary/hipster

Hipster - contemporary subculture (Wikipedia):
http://en.wikipedia.org/wiki/Hipster_%28contemporary_subculture%29

Generation Sell (The New York Times):
http://www.nytimes.com/2011/11/13/opinion/sunday/the-entrepreneurial-generation.html?pagewanted=all

Why the hipster must die (TimeOut):
http://www.timeout.com/newyork/things-to-do/why-the-hipster-must-die

The Man Who Gave Underwear Pockets

Danieal Underwear website:
http://www.danieal.com/

Danieal Underwear (Facebook):
https://www.facebook.com/livedanieal

The Jellyfish Entrepreneur

Jellyfish Art:
http://jellyfishart.com

Monterey Bay Aquarium:
http://www.montereybayaquarium.org/

Ocean Treasues SF:
http://oceantreasuressf.com

My startup makes jellyfish aquariums (Hacker News):
https://news.ycombinator.com/item?id=466497

Technology Start-Ups (NYT):
http://www.nytimes.com/2009/03/14/technology/start-ups/14startup.html?_r=0

Urinating on a Jellyfish Sting is Effective (Scientific American):
http://www.scientificamerican.com/article.cfm?id=fact-or-fiction-urinating

"Friends": The One with the Jellyfish (IMDb):
http://www.imdb.com/title/tt0583620/

Global Pet Expo 2011 - Showcase Winners:
http://globalpetexpo.org/press/pressrelease_detail.asp?id=92

Desktop Jellyfish Tank (Kickstarter):
http://www.kickstarter.com/projects/1497255984/desktop-jellyfish-tank

Chat Basket:
http://chatbasket.com/

The Van With No Plan

The Van With No Plan Blog:
http://www.thevanwithnoplan.com/our-adventures.html

The Van With No Plan (Facebook):
https://www.facebook.com/Thevanwithnoplan

Job Corps:
http://www.jobcorps.gov/home.aspx

Hurricane Sandy Recovery (FEMA):
https://www.fema.gov

The Roving Typist

I Am An Object Of Internet Ridicule, Ask Me Anything (The Awl):
http://www.theawl.com/2013/09/i-was-a-hated-hipster-meme-and-then-it-got-worse

Roving Typist:
https://rovingtypist.com/

A Story and a Picture:
http://astoryandapicture.com/

Spotted on the Highline (Reddit):
http://www.reddit.com/r/nyc/comments/ygfv7/spotted_on_the_highline/

It Happened To Me: I Got Dumped by a Meme (xoJane):
http://www.xojane.com/it-happened-to-me/it-happened-to-me-i-got-dumped-by-a-meme

Robot Dance Party

Robot! (YouTube):
http://www.youtube.com/watch?v=-FDgyT9V5nw

Maker Faire:
http://makerfaire.com/

Robot Dance Party:
http://robotdanceparty.org/

Coleridge on disbelief, Wordsworth on awakening (UT, Knoxville):
https://notes.utk.edu/Bio/greenberg.nsf/0/aa819a734ce9d34585256e0e00
717ab4

What Rhymes With Hug Me?:
http://whatrhymeswithhug.me/

Robot Dance Party! (Kickstarter):
https://www.kickstarter.com/projects/1266784019/robot-dance-party

The Man Who Smuggles Trader Joe's Into Canada

The Buddhahouse:
http://thebuddhahouse.com/

Point Roberts, Washington (Wikipedia):
http://en.wikipedia.org/wiki/Point_Roberts,_Washington

Aldi (Wikipedia):
http://en.wikipedia.org/wiki/Aldi

Gray Market Clobbered by Dollar Drop, Retailers Say (Los Angeles Times):
http://articles.latimes.com/1988-06-01/business/fi-3595_1_gray-market-
dealers

Supreme Court OKs Discounted Resale Of 'Gray Market' Goods (NPR):
http://www.npr.org/blogs/thetwo-way/2013/03/19/174757355/supreme-
court-oks-discounted-resale-of-gray-market-goods

Dumb Starbucks (Wikipedia):
http://en.wikipedia.org/wiki/Dumb_Starbucks

The Invention of the AeroPress

Flying disc (Wikipedia):
http://en.wikipedia.org/wiki/Frisbee

Edward "Steady Ed" Headrick (Find A Grave Memorial):
http://www.findagrave.com/cgi-bin/fg.cgi?page=gr&GRid=6684592

Payson man enters legendary sailing race (Payson Roundup):
http://www.paysonroundup.com/news/2007/jun/28/payson_man_enters
/?print

Shakuhachi (Wikipedia):
http://en.wikipedia.org/wiki/Shakuhachi

The Aerobie Book (John Cassidy):
http://www.amazon.com/The-Aerobie-Book-Investigation-Mini-Machine/dp/0932592309

Aerobie High Performance Sport Toys:
http://aerobie.com/

Lift (Wikipedia):
http://en.wikipedia.org/wiki/Lift_(force)

Parker Brothers (Wikipedia):
http://en.wikipedia.org/wiki/Parker_Brothers

Mother Lode Plasites:
http://www.mlplastics.com/

Airfoil (Wikipedia):
http://en.wikipedia.org/wiki/Airfoil

Faster, Farther, Fearless - Aerobie Takes On Frisbee (Chicago Tribune):
http://articles.chicagotribune.com/1986-10-29/business/8603210539_1_frisbee-alan-adler-aerobie

Is there a better frisbee than the aerobee in terms of distance? (Quora):
http://www.quora.com/Is-there-a-better-frisbee-than-the-aerobee-in-terms-of-distance

Quarter Mile Throw (Aerobie):
http://aerobie.com/about/news/quartermilethrow.htm

AEROPRESS:
http://www.aeropress.ca/

Melitta:
https://www.melitta.com/

Machines and Brewing Methods (CoffeeGeek):
http://coffeegeek.com/forums/coffee/machines/195166?LastView=1393436826&Page=2

Coffee Fest:
https://www.coffeefest.com/

Aeropress Coffee and Espresso Maker (Amazon):
http://www.amazon.com/gp/product/B0047BIWSK/ref=as_li_tf_tl?ie=UTF8&tag=aerinc-20&linkCode=as2&camp=217145&creative=399369&creativeASIN=B0047BIWSK

CoffeeGeek:
http://coffeegeek.com/

World Aeropress Championships:
http://worldaeropresschampionship.com/

S Filter - A Reusable Coffee Filter for AeroPress (Kickstarter):
https://www.kickstarter.com/projects/kaffeologie/s-filter-a-reusable-coffee-filter-for-aeropress

Able Brewing Travel Cap for Aeropress (Bytown Beanery):
http://bytownbeanery.wordpress.com/able-brewing-travel-cap-for-aeropress/

AeroPress Brewstation (Espresso Deco):
http://espressodeco.com/aeropress-brewstation

Updated Aeropress brewing method (Coffee Collective):
http://coffeecollective.blogspot.com/2010/01/updated-aeropress-brewing-method.html

Slapsie (Copyright Encyclopedia):
http://www.copyrightencyclopedia.com/slapsie-the-pull-apart-put-together-fun-in-motion-toy/

The Man Who Sees Art in Cheetos

Cheese Curls of Instagram:
http://instagram.com/cheesecurlsofinstagram?modal=true

Cheese Curl Art (Etsy):
https://www.etsy.com/shop/CheeseCurlArt

Food Truck Economics

Phat Thai SF:
http://phatthaisf.com/

Wholesale Food Service Equipment (Restaurant Depot):
http://www.restaurantdepot.com/

About (Mission Dispatch):
http://missiondispatchsf.com/about/

Off the Grid:
http://offthegridsf.com

How Social Media Is Fueling the Food Truck Phenomenon (Mashable):
http://mashable.com/2011/06/16/food-trucks-social-media/

Filming On Location: San Francisco on May 7-13 (EatSt.):
http://eatst.foodnetwork.ca/blog/eat-st-filming-on-location-san-francisco-
on-may-7-13.html

Food Trucks as Lean Startups (Small Business Labs):
http://www.smallbizlabs.com/2012/07/food-trucks-as-lean-startups.html

Lean startup (Wikipedia):
http://en.wikipedia.org/wiki/Lean_Startup

Old World Food Truck:
http://www.oldworldfoodtruck.com/

The Restaurant Failure Myth (Businessweek):
http://www.businessweek.com/stories/2007-04-16/the-restaurant-failure-
mythbusinessweek-business-news-stock-market-and-financial-advice

How Independent Operators Finance Restaurants (Restaurant Owner):
http://www.restaurantowner.com/public/782.cfm%20

SOMA StrEat Food Park:
http://somastreatfoodpark.com/

Armenco Hot Dog Cart Manufacturing Company:
http://www.cateringtruck.com/used.html

Instrucktional:
http://instrucktional.com/

San Francisco Incubator Kitchen (La Cocina):
http://www.lacocinasf.org/

We Love Food Trucks (Mobi Munch):
http://www.mobimunch.com/

Construction Guys Never Ate Like This (Macleans):
http://www2.macleans.ca/2010/09/30/construction-guys/

The Great Food Truck Race (Food Network):
http://www.foodnetwork.com/the-great-food-truck-race/index.html

Street Vendors in the US (IBISWorld):
http://www.ibisworld.com/industry/default.aspx?indid=1683

Food Trucks Battle Restaurants Over Street Space (WSJ):
http://online.wsj.com/article/SB10000872396390443404004577576992254177540.html

Proposed New Food Truck Rules (San Francisco Examiner):
http://www.sfexaminer.com/local/2013/01/proposed-new-food-truck-
rules-san-francisco-seek-please-both-mobile-and-stationary-eat

Me So Hungry Food Truck:
http://mesohungrytruck.com/

San Francisco Food Trucks Tired of Fighting for Permits (Biz Journals):
http://upstart.bizjournals.com/companies/startups/2012/09/26/san-francisco-food-trucks-band-together.html?page=all

Chef Pelle:
http://chefpelle.com/

One Nation Under Pod (Portland Mercury):
http://www.portlandmercury.com/portland/one-nation-under-pod/Content?oid=4163268

Why Food Trucks Aren't Going Away (TIME):
http://ideas.time.com/2012/06/13/food-trucks-are-here-to-stay/

Revenue That Comes With Selling Alcohol (Chron.com):
http://smallbusiness.chron.com/revenue-comes-selling-alcohol-34021.html

How to Price Alcoholic Beverages in Your Bar or Restaurant (FSW):
http://www.foodservicewarehouse.com/education/how-to-price-alcoholic-beverages-in-your-bar-or-restaurant/c27452.aspx

Top 5 food mark-ups where restaurants make huge profits (DailyFinance):
http://www.dailyfinance.com/2010/09/08/top-5-food-mark-ups-where-restaurants-make-huge-profits/

Curry Up Now:
http://www.curryupnow.com/restaurants

The Saga of Yoga Joes

Yoga Poses, Classes, Meditation, and Life (Yoga Journal):
http://www.yogajournal.com/press/yoga_in_america

Has Yoga Become Too Commercialized? (Elle):
http://www.elle.com/beauty/health-fitness/commercialization-of-yoga-2

Brogamats:
http://brogamats.com/

Spreadable Butter - advertising Portfolio:
http://spreadablebutter.com/

ellaprint (PromoPlace):
http://www.promoplace.com/ellaprint/

So I just designed some yoga mats for dudes (Reddit):
http://www.reddit.com/r/yoga/comments/102pkv/so_i_just_designed_some_yoga_mats_for_dudes/

Yoga Joes (Kickstarter):
https://www.kickstarter.com/projects/241445217/yoga-joes-army-men-doing-yoga

Stephanie Stolorow Yoga:
http://www.stephaniestolorow.com/

Moddler:
http://www.moddler.com/

Rapid Injection Molding (FATHOM):
http://studiofathom.com/rapid-prototyping/advanced-rapid-injection-molding/

Research on Yoga and PTSD (Warriors At Ease):
http://warriorsatease.com/resources/research/

Life as a LEGO Professional

Ole Kirk Christiansen (Wikipedia):
http://en.wikipedia.org/wiki/Ole_Kirk_Christiansen

Lego (Wikipedia):
http://en.wikipedia.org/wiki/Lego

Star Wars Ultimate Collector Millennium Falcon (eBay):
http://www.ebay.com/itm/NEW-LEGO-10179-Star-Wars-Ultimate-Collectors-Millennium-Falcon-/191093977032?pt=Building_Toys_US&hash=item2c7e16afc8

Lego Master Builder Interview (Yahoo):
http://news.yahoo.com/blogs/movie-news/lego-master-builder-interview-220617918.html

Become the next Master Model Builder (LEGOLAND):
http://www.legolanddiscoverycenter.com/boston/brickfactor/

Recent UT grad named Lego master model builder (Reporter News):
http://www.reporternews.com/news/2011/jan/24/recent-ut-grad-namedlego-master-model-builder/?print=1

What is a LEGO Master Builder? (LEGO):
http://mba.lego.com/en-us/guide/what-is-a-lego-master-builder

Dirk Denoyelle (amazings.eu):
http://www.amazings.eu/index.php?id=55

LEGO Certified Professionals (LEGO):
http://aboutus.lego.com/en-us/lego-group/programs-and-visits/lego-certified-professionals

Master Lego Model Builder (Apprentice Power):
http://www.apprenticepower.com.au/hints-and-tips/wicked-weird-and-wanted-jobs-master-lego-model-builder/

How does one become a LEGO Certified Professional? (Quora):
http://www.quora.com/LEGO/How-does-one-become-a-LEGO-Certified-Professional

Nathan Sawaya - The Art of the Brick:
http://brickartist.com/about/

Fulfilling a Kid's Dream to Play With Legos All Your Life (WSJ):
http://online.wsj.com/news/articles/SB1000142405297020350320457703
8164225658328

Brickville DesignWorks:
http://www.brickville.ca/#xlink

Sean Kenney - Art with LEGO bricks:
http://www.seankenney.com/

Milton Train Works - KCCUSA Summer Block Party:
http://miltontrainworks.com/MTW/services/KCC/

Brickmania Track Links (Kickstarter):
https://www.kickstarter.com/projects/brickmania/brickmania-track-links-custom-add-on-for-the-lego

Brickpicker:
http://www.brickpicker.com/

BrickLink:
http://www.bricklink.com/

Brickset:
http://brickset.com/

The Cheeseboard Collective

The Cheese Board Collective:
http://www.cheeseboardcollective.coop/

The Cheese Board Collective Works (Cheese Board Collective Staff):
http://www.amazon.com/The-Cheese-Board-Collective-Pastry/dp/1580084192

Cheese Board Pizza (Yelp):
http://www.yelp.com/biz/cheese-board-pizza-berkeley?start=120

Alice Waters (Wikipedia):
http://en.wikipedia.org/wiki/Alice_Waters

Alice Waters and Chez Panisse (Thomas McNamee):
http://www.amazon.com/Alice-Waters-Panisse-Thomas-McNamee/dp/0143113089

Alice Waters: Food Pioneer (Makers):
http://www.makers.com/alice-waters

Arizmendi - Lakeshore:
http://arizmendilakeshore.com/

Arizmendi Association of Cooperatives:
http://www.arizmendi.coop/

Arizmendi Serving Up Jobs With Ownership in the Mission (Mission Local):
http://missionlocal.org/2010/09/arizmendi-serving-up-jobs-with-ownership-in-the-mission/

Why the Lucky Stiff

Where's _why? (Slate):
http://www.slate.com/articles/technology/technology/2012/03/ruby_ruby_on_rails_and__why_the_disappearance_of_one_of_the_world_s_most_beloved_computer_programmers_.html

_Why: A Tale of a Post-Modern Genius (Smashing Magazine):
http://www.smashingmagazine.com/2010/05/15/why-a-tale-of-a-post-modern-genius/

_why resurfaces, disappears again (venturebeat):
http://venturebeat.com/2013/04/19/why-oh-why/

Why's Complete Printer Spool (Internet Archive):
https://archive.org/details/136875051WhySCompletePrinterSpoolAsOneBook

Why's (Poignant) Guide to Ruby (Why the Lucky Stiff):
http://mislav.uniqpath.com/poignant-guide/

Starting a Bike Shop

Startup = Growth (Paul Graham):
http://paulgraham.com/growth.html

Class 4 Notes Essay (Peter Thiel):
http://blakemasters.com/post/21169325300/peter-thiels-cs183-startup-class-4-notes-essay

Huckleberry Bicycles:
http://www.huckleberrybicycles.com/

San Francisco Office of Economic and Workforce Development:
http://www6.sfgov.org/index.aspx?page=134

Want to Start a Bike Shop? (National Bicycle Dealers Association):
http://nbda.com/articles/want-to-start-a-bike-shop-pg70.htm

POS Software:
http://merchantos.com/

The Man Who Gives Half His Work Away For Free

Very Nice Co:
http://verynice.co/

How to Give Half Your Work Away For Free (Matthew Manos):
http://givehalf.co/

Social Design (Wikipedia):
http://en.wikipedia.org/wiki/Social_design

Why Nonprofits Should Invest More in Advertising (HBR):
http://blogs.hbr.org/2009/05/why-nonprofits-should-spend-mo/

Savage County Poster (verynice):
  http://verynice.co/wpcontent/uploads/2013/12/SavageCounty_Poster_00
1.jpg

How to Give Half Your Work Away For Free (Indiegogo):
https://www.indiegogo.com/projects/how-to-give-half-of-your-work-away-
for-free

The Leather Craftsman

The Art of Hand Sewing Leather (Al Stohlman):
http://www.amazon.com/The-Art-Hand-Sewing-Leather/dp/1892214911

Neo Nouveau:
http://neonouveau.ca/

History of Leather (Leather Resource):
http://www.leatherresource.com/history.html

Picked up some alligator and made a 5-figure briefcase by hand. (Reddit):
http://www.reddit.com/r/malefashionadvice/comments/1qejdt/picked_up
_some_alligator_and_made_a_5figure/

Nina G: The Stand-Up Comedian Who Stutters

Nina G. - Comedian:
http://www.ninagcomedian.com/

National Stuttering Association:
http://www.westutter.org/

Stand Ups and Their Salaries (New York Times):
http://www.nytimes.com/2012/11/04/arts/stand-ups-and-their-
salaries.html?pagewanted=all&_r=1&

Nina G. (YouTube):
http://www.youtube.com/user/ninagcomic

Once Upon An Accommodation (Nina G., Mean Dave):
http://www.amazon.com/Once-Upon-An-Accommodation-
Disabilities/dp/1482554445/

The Chocolate Hacker

Firefly Chocolate:
http://fireflychocolate.com/

From Bean to Bar: Dark Chocolate from Scratch (Instructables):
http://www.instructables.com/id/From-Bean-to-Bar-Dark-Chocolate-from-
Scratch/

Firefly Chocolate - Tilt:
https://fireflychocolate.tilt.com

America's First Not-for-Profit Bar

Rachel Hadiashar Photography:
http://rachelhadiashar.com/

The Oregon Public House:
http://oregonpublichouse.com/

Okra:
http://www.friedokra.org/charity-bar.html

Shebeen:
http://www.shebeen.com.au/

Causedc.org:
http://www.causedc.org/

Oregon Boasts Strong Nonprofit Sector (Eugene Register-Guard):
http://news.google.com/newspapers?
nid=1310&dat=20080120&id=EmFWAAAAIBAJ&sjid=mPADAAAAIBAJ&
pg=6798,3860663

Oregon Public House combines beer with charity (OregonLive.com):
http://www.oregonlive.com/living/index.ssf/2013/05/oregon_public_hous
e_combines_b.html

In New Pubs, Good Cheer and Good Works (New York Times):
http://www.nytimes.com/2013/01/21/us/new-pubs-send-profits-to-charity.html?_r=1&

Whole Foods Market:
http://www.wholefoodsmarket.com/mission-values/caring-communities/community-giving

The Restaurant-Failure Myth (Businessweek):
http://www.businessweek.com/stories/2007-04-16/the-restaurant-failure-mythbusinessweek-business-news-stock-market-and-financial-advice

Portland Brew Pubs and Microbreweries (10Best):
http://www.10best.com/destinations/oregon/portland/nightlife/brew-pubs/

Benefit Corporation:
http://benefitcorp.net/

Ageusia (Wikipedia):
http://en.wikipedia.org/wiki/Ageusia

The Truth About Ben & Jerry's (Stanford Social Innovation Review):
http://www.ssireview.org/articles/entry/the_truth_about_ben_and_jerrys

Ben & Jerry's (Wikipedia):
http://en.wikipedia.org/wiki/Ben_%26_Jerry's

Unilever:
http://www.unilever.com/

Beneficial Banking:
http://www.onepacificcoastbank.com/

How Many Benefit Corporations Have Been Formed? (socentlaw):
http://socentlaw.com/2013/07/how-many-benefit-corporations-have-been-formed/

Kyle Westaway (socentlaw):
http://socentlaw.com/author/kylewes/

Exploring the Role Delaware Plays as a Domestic Tax Haven (Scott Dyreng, Bradley P. Lindsey, Jacob R. Thornock) :
http://papers.ssrn.com/sol3/papers.cfm?abstract_id=1737937

Socially responsible investing (Wikipedia):
http://en.wikipedia.org/wiki/Socially_responsible_investing

The Forum for Sustainable and Responsible Investment:
http://www.ussif.org/content.asp?contentid=82

Drive: The Surprising Truth About What Motivates Us (Daniel H. Pink):
http://www.amazon.com/Drive-Surprising-Truth-About-
Motivates/dp/1594484805

The Underground Economy of Dolores Park

Dolores Park's many fans come up with an overhaul (SFGate):
http://www.sfgate.com/bayarea/article/Dolores-Park-s-many-fans-come-
up-with-an-overhaul-3407550.php

The Really Really Free Market:
http://www.reallyreallyfree.org/

Dolores Park History (Dolores Park Works):
http://www.doloresparkworks.org/dolores-park-renovation/park-history/

Vandalism at San Francisco Cemeteries:
http://www.sanfranciscocemeteries.com/vandalism.html

Real Estate Owned by the City and County of San Francisco (Board of
Supervisors):
http://books.google.com/books?id=VfcsAAAAYAAJ&dq=san%20francisco
%20%22Mission%20Park%22&pg=PA101#v=onepage&q=san%20francisco
%20%22Mission%20Park%22&f=false

Dolores Park: A Historical Landmark? (Mission Local):
http://missionlocal.org/2011/09/wait-dolores-park-is-historical/

San Francisco Call (California Digital Newspaper Collection):
http://cdnc.ucr.edu/cgi-bin/cdnc?a=cl&cl=CL1&sp=SFC

The Great 1906 San Francisco Earthquake (USGS):
http://earthquake.usgs.gov/regional/nca/1906/18april/index.php

Dolo Rehab Nutshell (Dolores Park Works):
http://www.doloresparkworks.org/2013/11/dolo-rehab-nutshell/

Annual report of the Department of Public Health:
https://archive.org/details/annualreportofde19101911sanf

Apple Maps Blows Up Dolores Park Truffle Guy's Spot (SFist):
http://sfist.com/2012/11/26/apple_maps_blows_up_pot_truffle_guy.php

Not Cool: Ganja Treat Man Arrested in Dolores Park! (SFist):
http://sfist.com/2012/09/11/update_from_the_war_on_fun_ganja_tr.php

New Dolores Park food vendor: Costco pizza guy (Mission Mission):
http://www.missionmission.org/2012/07/22/new-dolores-park-food-
vendor-costco-pizza-guy/

Cold Beer, Huge Profits (Uptown Almanac):
http://uptownalmanac.com/2011/02/cold-beer-huge-profits

COLD BEER COLD WATER ARRESTED (Uptown Almanac):
http://uptownalmanac.com/2012/04/cold-beer-cold-water-arrested

missionhipsters:
http://missionhipsters.com/

They Hatin': Ganja Treats Man Bust Followup (Uptown Almanac):
http://uptownalmanac.com/2010/03/they-hatin-ganja-treats-man-bust-followup

The Founding of Hacker School

Hackruiter (YC S10) Launches Hacker School (Hacker News):
https://news.ycombinator.com/item?id=3435183

"Good On Video" Is The New "Good On Paper" (TechCrunch):
http://techcrunch.com/2010/08/02/good-on-video-is-the-new-good-on-paper-with-ycombinators-hirehive-and-ycommonapp/

Hacker School:
https://www.hackerschool.com/

The Business of Phish

Mr. Miner's Greek Mythology (Phish Thoughts):
http://phishthoughts.com/2010/08/06/the-greek-mythology/

Phish Band Statistics (Statistic Brain):
http://www.statisticbrain.com/phish-band-statistics/

Phish | Awards (AllMusic):
http://www.allmusic.com/artist/phish-mn0000333464/awards

Phish.net:
http://phish.net/song/

Down with Disease - Beavis and Butthead (YouTube):
http://www.youtube.com/watch?v=anAXAy9M5VM

Entrepreneurship (Wikipedia):
http://en.wikipedia.org/wiki/Bootstrapping_(business)#Financial_Bootstrapping

A Rare Look at Phish as a Five Piece (Hidden Track):
http://www.glidemagazine.com/hiddentrack/a-rare-look-at-phish-as-a-five-piece/

Phish -(Wikipedia):
http://en.wikipedia.org/wiki/Phish

Outliers (Malcolm Gladwell):
http://en.wikipedia.org/wiki/Outliers_(book)

Phish: The Biography (Parke Puterbaugh):
http://www.amazon.com/Phish-The-Biography-Parke-
Puterbaugh/dp/B004Q7E252

The Phish Companion (Mockingbird Foundation):
http://www.amazon.com/The-Phish-Companion-Guide-
their/dp/0879306319

Phish - Why did Trey get kicked out of school? (Phantasy Tour):
http://phantasytour.com/bands/1/topics/2601029/posts

Trey Anastatio Interview (High Times):
http://hightimes.com/entertainment/jchesham/893

Phish - Bouncing Around the Room, 1990 (YouTube):
http://www.youtube.com/watch?v=EfdcHOtAxhY

Frodo Forever:
http://www.frodoforever.com/tree.php

Gamehendge (Wikipedia):
http://en.wikipedia.org/wiki/Gamehendge

Frequently Asked Questions (Phish.net):
http://phish.net/faq/what-and-where-is-the-rhombus

Phish Ring In The New Year (Adam Handman):
http://www.adamhandman.com/post/2554629097/shocks-my-brain-
phish-ring-in-the-new-year

Ham and Potatoes (Starving Kitten):
http://starvingkitten.com/2010/04/09/ham-and-potatoes/

MSG Commemorative Tokens (Phish.net):
http://blog.phish.net/1316932565/msg-commemorative-tokens

Phish discography (Wikipedia):
http://en.wikipedia.org/wiki/Phish_discography

15 Must-Hear Shows for Any Phish Novice (LIVE music blog):
http://livemusicblog.com/2010/07/23/phish-friday-15-must-hear-shows-
for-any-phish-novice/

ABOUT THE AUTHORS

Priceonomics is a San Francisco-based company that writes stories about innovators and economics, and also provides data services for businesses. The authors of this book are:

Rohin Dhar
Rohin is a new dad. He likes to ride bikes and drink coffee. He holds an MBA from Stanford and BA from Dartmouth.

Zachary Crockett
Zack plays many stringed instruments, climbs mountains, and is working on a collection of South American travel narratives.

Rosie Cima
Rosie can usually be found making slow progress on several different music, digital art, and literature projects at a time, and generally tuckering herself out. She likes punk rock shows.

Alex Mayyasi
Alex enjoys hiking, good food, and the rare days when the San Francisco fog lifts. He is writing a book about the Egyptian Revolution.

Hipster Business Models also features cover artwork by the multi-talented **Dan Abramson**.

CPSIA information can be obtained at www.ICGtesting.com
Printed in the USA
LVOW11s2005260315

432162LV00003B/92/P

STRENGTHENING YOUR FAITH

Teachings from John's Gospel

GREG LAURIE

 Dana Point, California

Strengthening Your Faith

ISBN 0-9762400-7-6

Printed in Canada.

Published by: Kerygma Publishing—Dana Point, California
Coordination: FM Management, Ltd.
Cover design: Christopher Laurie
Editing: Karla Pedrow
Interior Design: Highgate Cross+Cathey, Ltd.